W9-CXL-995

Gospel Essays

Gospel Essays

Frontier of Sacred and Secular

Mark C. Kiley

WIPF & STOCK · Eugene, Oregon

GOSPEL ESSAYS
Frontier of Sacred and Secular

Wipf & Stock
An Imprint of Wipf and Stock Publishers
199 W. 8th Ave., Suite 3
Eugene, OR 97401
www.wipfandstock.com

ISBN 13: 978-1-61097-983-2
Manufactured in the U.S.A.

To tomorrow's researchers
in New Testament and Christian Origins

He who translates a verse with strict literalness is a falsifier.
He who makes additions to it is a blasphemer.

—TOSEFTA MEGILLAH 3:21

Contents

Foreword

THE SET OF ESSAYS collected here is no ordinary introduction to gospel study. Each chapter presents not an overall view but a carefully selected perspective from which to approach the text.

Mathematicians, agriculturists, musicians, poets, and many others lend their expertise in these pages to new and creatively imaginative interpretations that will enrich the reader's understanding of the multiple layers of associations and possibilities available in biblical narratives.

These are exercises in playful intuitive imagination that provide layer upon layer of rich associations. Plays on words and numbers from Hebrew, Greek, and Latin sources, more often seen in rabbinic than in Western biblical exegesis, enliven the expositions and reveal the author's wide knowledge of biblical and classical sources.

It is to be hoped that the reader of these essays will come away with a wider and deeper sense of interpretive traditions and of the possibilities for contemporary interpretation of these foundational texts.

Carolyn Osiek, R.S.C.J.
Charles Fischer Catholic Professor, *Emerita*
Brite Divinity School at Texas Christian University
January 30, 2012

Preface

THIS IS A LITTLE pocket book, a *vade mecum*. In a general sense, I intend it to be read by anyone looking for something substantive to read in transit, to complement the larger journeys in which he or she is engaged. But it is also appropriate for use in communal settings that engage in advanced Biblical studies. These Gospel essays reflect my distilled dialogue with the sacred texts as well as with some relevant scholarship, where it exists. As a group, the articles bring the reader to what I hope is a more satisfying understanding of the texts in their primary settings, whose linguistic and cultural parameters were set by Hebrew, Greek, and Latin. In so doing they redress some of the imbalance in current theological work in the American Catholic academy in particular: Matthew Lamb has suggested that during the latter two decades of the twentieth century, approximately 90 percent of doctoral dissertations at Catholic universities dealt with issues arising from within the nineteenth and twentieth centuries. After reading the essays at hand, the reader will have tasted some of the exhilaration of watching inspired Evangelists contribute their Hellenistic word to the received mystery of God in Christ. I find it a taste that is never cloying. I hope that you will too.

Of the many to whom this applies, I am grateful to three colleagues in Biblical Studies who read and commented on these essays at earlier stages of their development: Tom Stegman SJ of Boston College, Vincent Pizzuto of the University of San Francisco, and John Clabeaux of Blessed Pope John XXIII Seminary in Massachusetts. John saved me from some factual errors and any that remain are my fault alone. I wish also to recognize the invaluable contribution of people in the local scene who have made possible the production of this booklet: the librarians of St. John's University on both of its New York campuses, but especially Joan Daly and Ginny Salvione in Staten Island, as well as the competent and generous graduate assistants provided by the University. My thanks go as well to the librarians of Wagner College, Staten Island, to the staffs of the St. Mark's Library of General Theological Seminary in Manhattan, the librarians of Bobst Library at New York University, the New York Public Library, and Columbia University's Burke and Butler libraries. They fulfill some of the promise inherent in the designation *Humanities*.

Perhaps most intriguing are the suggestions I have pursued that have been made with pictorial and audial subtlety and wit by some of my fellow New Yorkers. This group is the hardest to thank since they have chosen to remain anonymous. The Apple is full of dedicated readers who remain committed to the proposition that New York is less a city than a gigantic stage.

Mark Kiley
St. John's University
Staten Island campus
Jan. 18, 2012

Introduction

THE FIRST ESSAY, ON Matthew, suggests that the opening genealogy, presented in 3 groups of 14, helps set the agenda for the
Gospel as a whole. I make a case that 3.14 . . . , or pi, is an organizing principle for much of the text. This thesis respects the notion
that, at one level of abstraction, a circle has neither beginning nor
end, and that its determinate dimensions, reflected in pi, served
Matthew as a useful symbol of the life of God who is "with us" in
Christ. Inasmuch as this aspect of Matthew displays a dialogue
with the world of secular learning in its articulation of the gospel,
it serves as a model for the kind of learned engagement with Hebrew and Latin culture evidenced by the other Gospels.

The second essay, on Matthew 28's "phylacteries and fringes,"
sees the imagery of those Jewish artifacts as a guiding principle
in the Evangelist's final articulation of Jesus as embodied Torah.

The article on Mark suggests that this Gospel's relatively
long rendition of the execution of John the Baptist offers an aural
portrait of the lethal dynamics present in Genesis 3. I propose
that the Evangelist offers a hint, no more, that John is near the
heel of the new humanity, and bitten by a serpent whose persistent hissing fills the air of Herod's banquet.

The essay on Luke's infancy narratives explores some of the
Hebrew dynamics whereby the infancy narrative is textured. Pss.
15–24, containing an entrance liturgy at the Jerusalem Temple,
as well as words beginning with Hebrew 'ayin, stand behind a
significant portion of the Greek. Luke's variation of this entrance
liturgy prepares the hearers for a gospel account that juxtaposes
seeking the face of God with seeking Jesus. The Lukan essay finds
echo in the article on John 20, where that group of Psalms called

the Songs of Ascent plays a discernible role in John's presentation of Jesus glorified.

The article on John's Latinity attends to some of the literary parallels, grammatical structures, and vocabulary that help shape the Fourth Gospel, taking its cue in part from the unique notice in John 19 that the *titulus* on Jesus' cross was written in Latin as well as Hebrew and Greek. With the article on Luke, it traces some of the lexical logic of the Logos. That is, I suggest that the Fourth Evangelist takes up clusters of words, in this case in the Latin lexicon, and incorporates them in the presentation of Jesus the Word. Using John 4 as a test field, I also explore some of the relation of these Latinate dynamics to theological topics such as virtue, ecumenism and the Eucharist. Perhaps it will be the Trinitarian reflections that will be found most immediately useful in ongoing ecumenical reflections in the church.

The article on John 20 suggests, in a counterintuitive fashion, that the mystery of Jesus-lifted-up is presented here in ways that mimic the musical profile of Paul's description of the gift of tongues (1 Cor 14). In addition, the oddity of some details of Jesus' interaction with Mary Magdalene and the male disciples is best seen in light of the precise formulations in 1 Cor 14 about God-in-Christ. John 20 presents us with the mystery of Jesus Christ, head and members, glorifying God for what transpires in and through Jesus.

The essay on Acts is a natural extension of the Latinate dynamics in John. It examines some of the parallels between Acts 4–8 and Virgil's *Georgics*. As such, it complements some of the groundbreaking work done since the turn of the millennium concerning Luke's sustained engagement with the *Aeneid*.

one

Matthew's Pi

COME WITH ME TO Alexandria, Egypt where it is 150 BCE. Over a century has passed since a local luminary named Euclid offered three postulates that uncover principles of constructing with a circle and a straight line. And Archimedes, native of Syracuse who came to study in Alexandria, used those postulates to approximate the value of the relationship between a circle and its diameter, the line that cuts through the circle's middle. He set that value at 22/7 or 3.14 plus . . . . Such a value was of intense interest, because at one level of abstraction, a circle has neither beginning nor end, while the introduction of a diameter into a particular circle makes it possible to say something somewhat precise about an unknown quantity in either circle or line. Unbounded and precise. Can you hear the possibilities? Plato's dialogue Philebus, 15–18, had long since acknowledged the wisdom of attending to a unity not only in regard to the infinite but also with respect to specific numbers.[1] Our path turns now to the synagogue, where we witness Alexandrians who have for a century been rendering the Hebrew texts of their Sacred Scripture into Greek. When they plan their task, they so divide the Hebrew Psalter that they create a Psalm 31 that mentions *kyklos*, circle, not once, but twice (vss. 7 and 10 in the Greek version, the Septuagint, abbreviated LXX). The Septuagintal enumeration Ps. 31 is in itself an example of the relationship between infinity and limit.

---

1. Sumi, "The Species infima as the Infinite."

In what follows, we fast-forward to the end of the first century of the Common Era and inquire concerning those aspects of the Gospel of Matthew that might have been shaped by this heritage. We examine the cyclic traits of Matthew's Gospel in five parts: circle texts parallel to Matthew, circle and Pi within Matthew, the (circular) novelty of the adjective *oligopistos*, associated names-play within the Gospel, and the circular structure of the Gospel.

I. Circle Texts Parallel to Matthew

The very first verse of Psalm 31 (LXX) celebrates the forgiveness of *anomia*, lawlessness. The Evangelist four times uses this term in the Gospel (e.g. Matt 24:12 "as lawlessness increases, the love of many will grow cold"). Indeed, he is distinctive among the canonical Gospels in his frequent and original usage of this term.

The Matthean crucifixion, uniquely in the canon, includes an earthquake and a resurrection of some saints of Jerusalem (Matt 27:52, 53). Many commentators point out the seeming oddity of having their resurrection occur before that of Jesus. However, the most plausible explanation for the event may reside in Psalm 31:10 LXX "mercy will encircle (*kyklōsei*) the one who hopes in the Lord." Every commentator recognizes that the resurrection of the Matthean saints is similar to that of the dry bones in Ezekiel 37. But it is also noteworthy that the resurrection-vision in Ezekiel follows and reverses the lament "our hope is destroyed" (37:11). It seems that Matthew lobbed a volley of hope in Psalm 31:10 LXX toward its partner in Ezekiel 37, and that upon its return, this ricochet brought with it a corporate resurrection. Or, to put it differently, the hope that Matthew reads in Psalm 31 LXX rides the current of the encircling mercy of God. And by reading Ezekiel 37 through the lens of Psalm 31 LXX, the Evangelist asserts that at the cross of Jesus, the life without beginning or end is making a definitive appearance. All heaven is breaking loose, or a substantial foretaste thereof.

And Matthew is not alone in this regard. The other Gospels of the canon are in their distinctive ways as engaged with *kyklos* as is Matthew with Psalm 31. The Gospel of John uses the very next psalm after Psalm 31 that mentions *kyklo-*, that is, Psalm 33 (LXX), when John approximates the text by saying "not a bone of his will be broken" (John 19:21; Ps. 33:21 LXX). And Luke quotes Psalm 31 of the Hebrew enumeration when portraying Jesus as saying at the cross "Into your hands I commend my spirit" (Luke 23:46; Ps. 31:6). They may all have taken their Christian inspiration from the Gospel of Mark. There, the predicted time of the end of this age includes a darkening of the sun (13:24), which begins to transpire in the sun going dark at Jesus' cross (15:33). That crossover from this age to the new one is cradled within a text whose five occurrences of "time" (*kairos*) and counting off the hours of Jesus on the cross are congruent with Ps. 31:16 "My times are in your hands."

Apart from Psalm 31 LXX, one of the most wonderfully wrought aspects of Passion and Resurrection narratives in Matthew is centered in an exploration of Psalm 25 LXX in which the verb *kykloō* is employed: "I will wash my hands in innocence and go about/encircle your altar, Lord" (Ps. 25:6 LXX). Uniquely, in Matt 27:24, Pilate washes his hands before the crowd crying for Jesus' death. When, in the very next verse, Matt 27:25, the crowd calls down Jesus' blood on themselves and their children, we have an elaboration of Ps. 25:9 LXX in which the Psalmist asks for rescue from "men of blood / bloodthirsty men." But the parallels are more extensive yet. In Matt 28:12, the Evangelist explicitly states that the guards at the tomb were paid a large amount of money to spread a story about the disciples stealing Jesus' body to make it look like he had risen from the dead. Listen to Psalm 25:10 LXX: "their right hand is full of bribes." And finally, Psalm 25:12 LXX, the conclusion of the Psalm, has the Psalmist celebrate the fact that his "foot stands in an even place." Matt 28:9, uniquely among the Resurrection accounts of the canon, focuses on grasping the feet of the Risen One.

I would also offer the tentative suggestion that unique aspects of Matthew's Gospel are partly informed by a dialogue with a widely known text of antiquity itself constructed on cyclic repetitions, Homer's *Odyssey*. The encounter in Book 9 of Odysseus and the lawless Kyklōpes Polyphēmos presents us with themes that add texture to the attack of Jesus in Matt 23 on those who are blind guides, full of dead men's bones, disregarding the weightier matters of the law.

This dialogue may become quite sophisticated in Matt 26 if the uniquely Matthean word *dēlon* secondarily alludes to Dēlos, the center of the Cyclades Islands in the Aegean. The attendant in Matt 26:73 says to Peter that even your speech "makes you *dēlon*" (apparent; i.e. gives you away). Most commentators on the verse show a good deal of nervousness about our ability to demonstrate gradations of the spoken word in this period. But this scene with Peter occurs in the midst of others that contain echoes of book 5 of the *Odyssey*. Homer has Kalypso recount a tale of a mortal being hunted down by a god on Dēlos. This tale occurs in the midst of a talk with Hermes, who is depicted as able to put men to sleep by his power. The discourse ends when Kalypso acknowledges that there's no eluding the will of Zeus. These parallels-of-type are used by the Evangelist as texture in the springboard that ultimately propels the reader toward Peter's recognition of Jesus' identity in Matthew 16, bringing Peter to a position of central preeminence within the circle of Jesus' disciples. It is in Matthew 16 that Peter's speech also makes him *dēlon*, a center.

II. Circle and Pi within Matthew

Remembering that counting is inherent within the notion of scribe (*s-f-r*), allow me to offer some other exploratory suggestions about some of the most beautifully crafted dynamics of this literary circle:

The circle that forms the focus of this approach to Matthew should not be seen as asserting a cyclic view of history whereby history repeats itself forever. Rather, the circle is a symbol of God's life, made available to a world / an age that has an end: its transformation in the life of God. Here we note with many observers that, while Matthew claims to have given us fourteen generations in his third triad in chapter 1, in fact he has only given us thirteen. Matthew is living in the final age, made definitively so by the Paschal mystery of Jesus.

And where is the word circle as such? While there is no explicit use of *kyklos*, circle, in Matthew, it is the silent elephant plopped down in the middle of the room. Matthew alone among the canonical Gospels mentions the *ekklēsia*, church, which shares all of the consonants in *kyklos* (kls). Moreover, the three-fold occurrence of *ekklēsia* (16:18; twice in 18:17) is mirrored in the fact that Matthew has tripled Mark's single occurrence of *kyllos*, maimed (Matt 15:30, 31; 18:8). Jesus, whose authority to straighten crooked limbs is unlimited, already begins now what will come to fruition at the end of the age. Indeed, of all the various types of healings effected by Jesus, it is limb-straightening that most closely resembles the diameter of a circle in the relationship we are tracing.

The feeding of two different crowds in Matthew 14 and 15 reflect those in Mark, with one notable difference. The number of people fed, 5000 and 4000 respectively, is rendered with an additional note "not counting women and children." I see here a literary expression of the ongoing value of Pi beyond its first few digits. Obviously, the portrait of women and children is inherently a note of fecundity and continuation. And their function in relation to Pi is depicted by the sentences that precede and follow their appearance. Matthew 14:20 and 15:39 each contain 14 words.

The Gospel is rife with groupings of threes. Jack Kingsbury's 1988 Matthean commentary argued that the phrase "from that time on Jesus began to . . ." (4:17, 16:21) divides the text at its most basic level into three portions.[2] Plummer's 1956 commentary as

---

2. Kingsbury, *Matthew as Story*, 38–40.

well as that of Davies and Allison (1988) see many more carefully wrought triads in the text.[3] Those are easy enough to observe. But the multiplier effect supplied by the unbounded circle to the enumerated 3.14 . . . is perhaps the best way to appreciate the text's 42 occurrences of gē, earth (3 x 14 = 42).

When one plants two perpendicular lines within a circle so as to form a stylized cross, one has uncovered the rationale for the number of antitheses being set at six. When adding the value of Pi for each line, we arrive at something slightly larger than the number six (3.14 + 3.14= 6.28 . . .). And of course, the stylized cross so formed is a literary expression of the result of Jesus' antithetical assertions, i.e. the passion. The 84 occurrences (6 x 14) of *ouranoi*, heavens, is another Matthean refraction of Pi and would suggest that the life without beginning or end, symbolized in the circle, is being made continually available through the cross of Jesus.[4]

The concept of measurement is of course central to the appreciation of Pi. Metro, measure, in Matthew 7:2 is not unique to Matthew; it occurs in Mark as well. But the soft rhyme of mētēr, mother, enjoys a preponderant presence in Matthew. It occurs 27 times, a multiple of three. I think that it is most satisfying to hear echoes of Sophia/Wisdom here: Philo, in *The Worse Attacks the Better*, 54, says that one does well to consider Sophia a mother who brought the world to completion. Indeed, these 27 occurrences of mētēr are exactly mirrored in the Septuagint of Genesis where it occurs twenty-seven times, perhaps helping to suggest that Matthew's Jesus, functioning as Sophia, is effecting a new creation. But there is also in Matthew a unique and related preponderance of terms related to justice: the *dik-* root occurs twenty-seven times, including noun, adjectival, and verbal forms. This language has a moral dimension of some kind, to be

3. Plummer, St. Matthew, xix-xxi. Davies and Allison, A Critical and Exegetical Commentary on the Gospel According to St. Matthew, vol. 1, 58–72, 86–87.

4. Also see Pennington, *Heaven*.

sure, but in its sense of "true, correct," it limns the contours of the house being built by Jesus-Sophia along the lines of Proverbs 9:1.

The Sermon on the Mount may be seen as an exposition of 9 beatitudes, 6 antitheses, 3 practices, and an assortment of tagalong admonitions, to some degree elaborating the Lord's Prayer. I would suggest that the unbounded quality of the circle generates the multiples of three, and that the excess at the end of the three practices of prayer, fasting and giving alms is none other than a formal parallel to 3.14 . . ... This thesis is indirectly supported by the fact that 6:14, the saying about forgiveness immediately following the prayer, has 16 words. This 16, I venture, represents the value of Pi attendant upon the two diameters that form a cross in Matthew's circle: 3+1+4 and 3+1+4 =16.

Now let us circle back to the beginning of the text: we remember that commentators have long noted that there are three groups of what Matthew says are fourteen generations in Matthew 1. I see here a conscious iteration of 3.14... At one level, the opening of the Gospel announces the interaction of infinity and limitation. Ancillary to that program, the name David in the genealogy has a value of 14: The name in Hebrew daleth-waw-daleth has the numerical equivalent of $4 + 6 + 4 = 14$. The placement of the name David is rather carefully plotted throughout the rest of the text so that its middle waw, resembling the vertical pole of a cross, announces the Passion: That is, the tenth occurrence of the name David, analogous to counting off the daleth and waw, immediately precedes the announcement in ch. 16 of Jesus' passion in Jerusalem, David's city. Similarly, the sixth occurrence of the word *horos*, mountain, also precedes the first announcement of the cross. In short, the name David is important to the plotting of the announcements of the cross in David's city.

III. Oligopistos

Perhaps the single most trenchant piece of stylistic evidence in regard to circle-and-Pi in Matthew resides in the expression "of little faith." The adjective *oligopistos* does not occur previously in Greek, though Luke and Sextus Empiricus use it after Matthew. It is tempting to think that Matthew coined the phrase and set it in motion in the culture, but we cannot be sure that the Evangelist originated it. However, I think we can say something about its peculiar role in the text of the Gospel.

The adjective occurs four times (6:30, 8:26, 14:31, 16:8) with a nominal variant in 17:20. Seeing it writ large may help the reader to understand its heuristic value:

Oligopistos.

The 3.14 value of *Pi* is hinted at by the three circular omicrons as well as the *Pi* -combination in the heart of the word. Each one of the four occurrences exists in the midst of a question, and that prominent emphasis on 4 might seem, at first glance, to weaken any suggestion that the word points to circle-and-Pi in which 3 is so important. But the four instances of the adjective are not wholly uniform. For example, the singular address to Peter in 14:31 ends in epsilon, not omicron, and in that instance, the adjectival pattern of three omicrons is broken. Moreover, the first occurrence of the adjective, in 6:30, is part of a question that asks "how much more?" I would suggest that the textual dynamics as a whole indeed do hint at a value of three- and-some-leftover precisely in these attributes just mentioned. And when the Evangelist uses the noun form, *oligopistia*, containing just two omicrons, we are given a summary recapitulation of the concept of having little faith. Again, to emphasize the importance of the number of omicrons employed, I supply a chart:

How much more? 6:30	8:26	14:31	16:8
OOO	OOO	OO	OOO

The nominal form employed in a declarative statement at 17:20 comes after the previous set has been completed and, by its status as noun, does not disturb the alphanumeric game being played.

What is the point of this Matthean pattern? Perhaps the Evangelist is suggesting that even the lamentable lack of faith displayed by the disciples, while an impediment to their growth in given instances, is itself fully a part of their engagement with the revelatory process and in no sense leaves them out of the larger loop. The stylistics employed in the text underscore that ideological point.

IV. Associated Names-Play within Matthew

The name *Maththaios* bears within it two occurrences of the letter *theta*. That letter replicates the very structure of circle and diameter that we have been examining. Indeed, the double occurrence of theta is coordinate with the double mention of circle-words in Psalm 31 (LXX). And if modern Greek pronunciation is a reliable guide to pronunciation in the first century, the name was articulated as *Maththeos*, bearing within it the sound of *theos*, God. The specified eternity of the Matthean revelation inheres stylistically in the name under which the Gospel is presented to us.

Also, the names of Euclid and Archimedes and the legends attached to them provide one set of meaningful coordinates for aspects of Matthew's Gospel. The name Euclid (*Eukleidēs*) bears within it the root of the word for "keys" *kleidas* as they occur, uniquely, in Matthew 16:19. The Arch-component of Archimedes is present in 4:17 and 16:21, "From that time on Jesus began to . . . *ērxato.*" These verses mark the major transitions in the sweep of the narrative, inaugurating the public ministry and the movement toward Jerusalem. Moreover, when Archimedes celebrated the core of the discovery of specific gravity and buoyancy, he emerged from his bath and shouted "Eureka," I found it.

The power of this legend set a precedent against which one may read the excitement of the man finding treasure in a field (13:44), a uniquely Matthean parable.

V. Special M material
and the circular structure of Matthew

Jack Kingsbury and Peter Ellis have been vigorous proponents of the thesis that the center of Matthew's text resides in the parables of chapter 13.[5] They are guided in this suggestion by the alternation of narrative and discourse throughout the text. And Ellis speaks explicitly about a concentric structure to the Gospel. Their form-critical observations are sound enough, as far as they go. But remembering that counting is endemic to the function of a scribe allows one to highlight the Evangelist's interest in the circle yet again. When one counts the approximately 18,346 words of the Greek text, one arrives at a center very near 15:30, 31. In this numerical center, in 15:30, *kyllos*, crippled, is mentioned third in order of diseases healed. And in 15:31, the word *kyllos* occurs in a sentence containing 14 omicrons which are, of course, shaped like a circle: 3.14. This is very much the center of Matthew's circle, the center point on its diameter. Adjacent, in Matthew 15:29, the Evangelist has placed a reminder of Jesus' presence in *Galilaia*. That place name bears within it, in Hebrew, the meaning of circle. Moreover, the majority of the 16 occurrences of Galilaia reside at the end and in the beginning chapters of the Gospel. While I would insist that all of the action in Matthew is happening along the diameter of the circle, each event is being shaped by the larger circle of God's life itself.

I would also suggest that there is, in M material peculiar to this Gospel, a hint of the Evangelist's circular interest. In what follows, I list sections of the Gospel, all of which contain some special Matthean material prior to 15:30, 31, and that occur in

5. Kingsbury, *Gospel Interpretation*, 16–26. Ellis, *Matthew*, 10–13.

a slightly different form in the latter half of the text.[6] They function, I would suggest, as a complement to the narrative/discourse structure of Kingsbury and Ellis.

Chs.

- 1–4, 26–28 warning dreams, Joseph, Mary, Jeremiah, persecution of innocent; new life, angels, kingdoms of earth

- 5, 25 sitting and blessing

- 6, 24 trumpet

- 7, 23 warnings concerning the importance of adherence to Jesus' teaching and entry into the reign of heaven

- 8–10, 19–22 two blind healed

- 10–12, 18 two arches (a construct of circle and line): sword, reward, J Bap, punishment, yoke; greatest in reign, three sources of scandal, shepherd, two or three witnesses, greater debt

- 13, 17 transformation and parables of finding

- 14–16 feedings and Gentiles/leaven

- 15:31 numerical center

Why this circular arrangement of much of the M material? Perhaps the major feasts of the Jewish liturgical calendar lend us some assistance. The following chart illustrates my point:

PASSOVER

WEEKS

15:30

DAY OF ATONEMENT

BOOTHS

PASSOVER

---

6. More M material is tabulated in Davies & Allison, *St. Matthew*, 1.121-24.

This lineup reflects the progression of the Jewish liturgical calendar. Could we not see the text as a liturgical mediation of the timeless life of God made available in Jesus? We have in Matthew 2 events that mimic the Passover of Exodus: the visit of a deadly attack on the innocent, followed by exit from Egypt. Thus is inaugurated a series of events reminiscent of the Torah-and-sign combination in Exodus during which the covenant is cut (Matt 5–10). The first half of the Gospel culminates in the offering of loaves (Matt 14, 15), akin to the offering of the first fruits of the grain harvest at the Feast of Weeks. In Matt 16:22, after Jesus predicts for the first time his being killed in Jerusalem, the uniquely Matthean *hileōs* in the mouth of Peter mirrors the *hilaskomai* at the heart of the Yom Kippur ("Day of Atonement") service in Leviticus 16. Both words are predicated on the notion of mercy and presuppose the bloody sacrifice at the Holy of Holies in Jerusalem. The explicit mention of *skēnai*, booths, in 17:4 marks the beginning of an emphasis on some of the themes of Booths: Jesus' indwelling presence (18:20) or absence (23:38), as well as the ingathering of the Final Judgment (ch 25). And we come full circle in Matt 26–28 to events at Passover.

I have argued elsewhere that the Gospel functions as a literary presentation of Wisdom's seven-pillared house.[7] I think we can now say that this literary house, liturgically structured, is also a circular dwelling. Indeed, while it is true, as we observed earlier, that the k-l-s combination is shared between *kyklos* and *ekklēsia*, it is now time to observe that these two words share the exact same consonantal configuration: k-k-l-s. This is not to reduce the circle of God's life without beginning or end to the church alone. That would be contrary to the Gospel message that holds them in relation to but in tension with one another. We may, however, look at the *ekklēsia* as one designated venue in which believers repeatedly encounter Jesus abiding as the divine presence, as exactly what his initial title in chapter 1 implies: Emmanuel, God with us.

7. Kiley, "Law, Wisdom, and the Housing Crisis."

Conclusion

The Gospel of Matthew took shape in a world, both broadly Hellenistic and particularly Jewish, taking for granted the transcendent perfection of the circle. So persistent was this belief that, in the realm of natural sciences, it would cede its authority only after centuries of further thought and observation.[8] Eventually, observers arrived at the more accurate appreciation of the elliptical shape of the galaxy we see today. Newly invigorated by this Gospel's exploration of Pi, Matthean Christians today may surely continue to cherish this Gospel's transcendent circle imagery, and appreciate it for what it is. Pi acts as an organizing principle of the literary expression of Matthew's faith in "God with us," in Jesus crucified and risen in the Spirit.

But of course, that does not preclude appreciation of the hard work and creativity involved in the diverse and ever-changing array of intellectual work on the natural world as such. Such believers may be moved by a particularly poignant scene in the recent movie "Agora." Set in Alexandria at the beginning of the fifth century CE, the film depicts a version of the legend of Hypatia, philosopher and astronomer, whose questions and observations marked a step away from the classical fixation on perfect circles. When challenged on her authority to teach Christians and Jews of Alexandria who were politically in the ascendant, when explicitly criticized as merely a pagan and female to boot, she replies "Your faith does not allow you to question. I must."

8. Nebelsick, *Circles of God*, 23–41 and subsequent reviews. Narins, *The World of Mathematics*, 2001.

two

Find the Phylacteries and Fringes (Matt 28)

COMMENTATORS WIDELY AGREE THAT, apart from the announcement of Jesus' resurrection to the women at the tomb, Matthew 28 is a kind of *cadenza* in which the Evangelist displays material largely peculiar to his community to describe the risen Jesus as *God with us*. But it is the task of this essay to suggest additionally that the themes of remembering and seeing, drawn from parts of the Torah concerned with phylacteries and fringes, lend a thoroughgoing unity to the chapter. Introduced by the theme of remembering in 27:63, the twenty-eighth chapter spurs believers to remember in Jesus the incipient triumph of the dual command to love God, and neighbor as one's self. And Jesus' commission to all the nations in the final chapter is partly shaped by the description of the fringes.

The chapter that we examine divides neatly into four scenes: announcement at the tomb, encounter of the women and Jesus, the bribe given to the guard of soldiers, and the revelation to the Eleven. We turn first to a reading of the special Matthean material against the template of the phylacteries.

PHYLACTERIES

The Bible is silent about the contemporary practice of wearing two small containers of Scriptural quotes, bound by leather straps to the left arm and forehead during morning prayer. However, such practice is often understood to derive from a reading of Deuteronomy 6:8, 11:18; and Exodus 13:9, 16. These verses prescribe binding "these words as a sign upon your hand and a frontlet between your eyes." In their figurative sense, they enjoin on the hearer a focused remembrance of God's acts in liberating and shaping the nation in covenant. The first literary mention of the use of the physical containers is made in the Letter of Aristeas (200 BCE–CE 100). And Qumran has yielded a container for the head, having four compartments that include the Decalogue of Deuteronomy 5, as well as fragmentary evidence of hand containers constituted by just one compartment.[1] Other Scriptural texts, written on parchment within both capsules, include Exodus 13:1–10; 11–16; Deuteronomy 6:4–9; 11:13–21. Though Josephus knows the concept (Ant 4.8.13), and the term *phylaktērion* was before Matthew used of protective amulets, Matthew's use of the term may have been in his mind justified by the command in Exodus 13:10 to guard this law, *phylaxesthe ton nomon touton*. Commentators widely assume that the literary and archaeological evidence points to the identity of Greek phylacteries and Hebrew tefillin.

The complaint of Matthew 23:5 is the sole New Testament instance of the use of the term phylacteries:

> They do all their works in order to be seen by people;
> they extend their phylacteries *phylaktēria*
> and make large the fringes *kraspeda*.

There are some characteristics unique to Matthew that in hindsight constitute early hints of the ways in which phylactery imagery is transformed in ch. 28. For example, Matthew 16:19, 20 use the language of binding and loosing, and apply it to Peter's function in the community. And this is rightly seen by most commentators to refer to some sort of adjudicating function exercised by Peter within the community. But this is language

---

1. Adler,"Identifying Sectarian Characteristics," 82–83; Freedman, "Phylacteries," 5.368–70.

entirely appropriate to the putting on and taking off of phylacteries as well. The Evangelist also provides within the Passion narrative proper some hints that prepare for the upcoming transformation of the phylactery image in ch. 28. He proffers a unique notice that there was, at the cross, an inscription written over Jesus' head (27:37). And where might one see Matthew's adaptation of the theme of "guarding" that resides at the linguistic heart of the words *phylaktērion/phylassein*? Uniquely in this Gospel, there is extended attention to the action of securing the tomb and placing a guard there (Matt 27:62–66; 28:2–4). The following list outlines some of the other broad similarities between phylacteries and Matt 28:

Phylacteries	Matt 28
Two identical portions of Torah	identical message of angel and Jesus (Matt 28:5–7 and 28:10)
Two containers	two scenes about the tomb
Eleven letters in *fylaktērion*[3]	eleven disciples

Here, the reader who is already familiar with the current state of Matthean commentary may object that "the Eleven" is a clear reminder of the fate of Judas whose end was in keeping with Matthew's generally escalated interest in the theme of judgment, in this case a negative one. I agree wholeheartedly. However, that observation does little beyond furthering our appreciation of the Evangelist's engagement with history. As we have come to appreciate, however, Matthew is also a literary artisan. And it is the place of the Eleven within the larger mosaic of Matthew as a piece of literature that I attempt to make visible in these observations. This is a piece of literature imagining its way into some of the significance of the mystery of Jesus as raised from the dead. And that mystery beyond the confines of time and space dictates

2. The transliteration symbol f accurately represents the initial *ph-* in the Greek.

the more profound significance of whatever kernels of history are transmitted. We do well to remember that all commentators make note of the fact that the messages of the angel and of Jesus in the first part of the chapter are identical. The identical portions of Torah in the two phylacteries provide an intelligible context for this idiosyncrasy. Along the same line, the double attention to the empty tomb underscores the container that is being left behind even as its potential surrogate, the Eleven as a group, are brought into view.[3]

The following list highlights more specific parallels between Matthew 28 and a phylactery's incorporation of Deuteronomy, particularly noting its sixth chapter.

Phylacteries	*Matthew* 28
Deuteronomy cited	*deute* (Matt 28:6)
Deuteronomy 6:7 command and journey	Matthew 28:16, 19, 20 command and journey
Deuteronomy 6: 2, 3 be careful to observe all that is taught	Matthew 28:20
The Shema (Deut 6:4–5)	approximately 80 words in Matt 28:16–20, as in the discussion of the Shema in Matt 22:34–40

In addition, only Matthew complements his use of the word for tomb as place of remembrance, *mnēmeion*, with the word *taphos*. The Evangelist may intend the hearer to recall in these words aspects of the four verses prescribing phylactery- binding: *zikkārōn*, memorial, in Exodus 13:9 and *tōtāpōt*, frontlets, in Exodus 13:16; Deuteronomy 6:8; 11:8.

One further detail of Matthew 28 anticipates eventual written legislation about the phylacteries. They are never worn on the Sabbath, presumably because the Sabbath gathering and rest will

3. For one example of the church's wrestling with history and symbol, see Young "Alexandrian and Antiochene Exegesis."

itself induce the desired remembrance of God's acts. Matthew's grammar in 28:1 makes it abundantly clear that the Sabbath was completely over when the women came to the tomb.

The composite picture emerging here is one in which the donning of the phylactery, known in Matthew's culture, is taken up into a revelation of the inbreaking reign of the Son of Man. In this Matthean scenario, it is the disciples themselves who keep in remembrance, guard carefully, the preeminent embodiment of Torah, Jesus himself. And what he embodies is the twin commands of the Torah to love God with one's whole self and to love one's neighbor as one's self.

FRINGES

We turn now to a series of details that suggests the Evangelist's use of the fringes as a framework within which to explore the risen Jesus' identity.

The fringes or tassels (*kraspeda*) are to be worn on the four corners of one's outer garment (Deut 22:12). The act of seeing them serves as a reminder of the importance of doing all of the Lord's commands (Num 15:39).

In 28:17, as the disciples see Jesus, he introduces them to exactly four uses of the word *pas*, all.[4] They are carefully arranged so that the two middle instances are identical and the last of the four differs from the first only by the addition of sigma.

- *Pasa*
- *Panta*
- *Panta*
- *Pasas*

4. Bradley, Matthew: Poet, Historian, Dialectician, xvii–xxii and 167–69, claims that the Evangelist employs a purposeful dialectic tension between the universal and the particular when employing the id- root for seeing (Matt 28:17). In a related vein, Bradley claims that a sense of exclusion is at work when the Evangelist employs the ops- root for seeing (Matt 28:7, 10).

The closest parallel to the function of the fringes resides in the saying of Jesus in 28:20, the end of the Gospel ". . . keep all that I have commanded you."[5] And the broadly-encompassing extent of the vision, all authority, all peoples, all that I have commanded, and all days reflect the encompassing extent of the physical fringes on all corners of one's outer garment.

Matthew's specifications of the word *all* serve to recall the previous three scenes of the chapter and serve as a bridge to the time of the Gospel's hearers:

All authority	Matt 28:1–7—*Guard* placed by authorities, Roman and Jewish, ineffectual in stopping Jesus' rising
All nations	Matt 28:8–10—Women sent to communicate a message centered on *Galilee* of the Gentiles. (See Matt 4:15).
All commandments	Matt 28:11–15—Soldiers do as they were *instructed*.
All days	Matt 28:16–20—Extending into the time of the hearers.

I find it particularly interesting that what was said of the phylacteries and fringes in 23:5 evidences a certain symmetry with the second and fourth specifications of the word *all*:

5. There are also several instances of *pas*, though not precisely four, in Is 25:6–8 LXX. These verses describe an anticipated bequest to all the nations given on a mountain where God acts. There is at present no consensus on the identity of the mountain in Matthew 28, and I see every reason to include this Isaiah text, along with the description of the fringes, as having a formative influence on the shaping of Matthew 28:16–20.

Matt 28	Matt 23:5
All nations	phylacteries are *broadened*
All days	the fringes are *lengthened*

Conclusion

In Matt 28, the Evangelist is explicit in asserting that Jesus' disciples as a group knew both worship and doubt. I would suggest that the ambiguity of their experience resulted in part from remembering themselves as profoundly rooted in their Jewish heritage but increasingly able to see its transformation in their emerging vision of Jesus.[6]

Amidst that experience, they managed to articulate a coherent and refined statement about Jesus as risen. They remember him as the definitive embodiment of Torah, the One who commissions and accompanies them, as they guard his word.

It may be the case that Matthew did not consider the possibility that his statement could be used to denigrate the integrity of practicing Jews who continue to use the phylacteries and fringes. We cannot know that with any certainty. But we can say that it is for disciples of Jesus that this transformation of phylacteries and fringes is most meaningful, and would make most sense to those who are baptized. With *Nostra Aetate*, Catholic exegetes can remember the ongoing validity of Jewish faith and practice, even while affirming the contours of the vision that Matthew offers to the disciples, a unique and holistic vision of Jesus as raised from the dead.

---

6. The theme of Jesus' authority juxtaposed with the disciples' doubt, a frequent Matthean refrain, is explored thoroughly by Poplutz, "Verunsicherter Glaube."

three

Extending Hisspitality to the Word in Mark 6:14–29

Concerning Mark's account of the execution
of John the Baptizer, John Meier says:

> Mark's account supplies reliable independent confirma-
> tion of the most basic points of Josephus' report. Beyond
> those, Josephus is to be preferred for history; Mark is to
> be mined for tradition history and theological intent.[1]

JOSEPHUS ASSERTS THAT JOHN preached in the jurisdiction of
Herod Antipas, who had him killed. In this essay, I argue that
the serpent of Genesis 3, with some help from Pliny, functions to
hold together many of the details beyond the claim of Josephus.

The initial justification for turning to the text of Genesis
resides in the setting of the banquet from which Herod's order to
execute John proceeds. The banquet celebrated Herod's birthday
(*genesiois*).[2] And, since the narrator of the pericope is already engaged in a widely-recognized "flashback," one that entails echoes

---

1. Meier, *A Marginal Jew*, 175. The historical problems and suggested reso-
lutions have been reviewed more recently by Kraemer, "Implicating Herodias."
An extended study of John in the Marcan context may be found in Webb, *John
the Baptizer*, 51–55; 373–77.

2. The Herodians certainly threw birthday parties [Persius, *Saturus*, 5.180;
cited in Taylor, *The Immerser*, 247.] But the particular contours of this party do
not come to us from Persius.

of Esther and the prophet Elijah, it is no inordinate stretch to inquire into that initial Biblical account of an encounter between God's Word and its resistant addressees.

Where may we discern the presence of the serpent? Not, please note, in the supposed eroticism of the dance that triggers the order to execute. There is no explicit eroticism here. However, in the very legginess required by the dance, which is found *pleasing* (6:22), and which then leads to a sentence of grief and death, we have a wonderful variation of the template of Genesis 3. There the presumably erect serpent, after the announcement of a prohibition and prior to the curse which requires that it crawl in the dust all its days, points out what is *pleasing*, and begins a chain of events leading to a sentence of grief and death.[3] Matthew, one of Mark's first editors, severely shortened the text in order to make room for other issues in his Gospel. But he did add one telling phrase that let his auditors know that he is transmitting what the Marcan account intended to convey. He has the girl dance "in their midst" / *en tō mesō* (Matt 14:6), mirroring the location of the tree with its pleasing fruit (Gen 3:3).[4]

Another important congruity exists between the behavior of the Herodians as a group and the sentence pronounced against the serpent in Genesis 3:15. The Septuagint there reads:

> There will be enmity between you and the woman,
> Between your seed and her seed.
> It [her seed] will guard [*tērein*] your head,
> And you shall guard its heel.

When Philo (*Laws* 3.189) comments on the verse, he notes that *tērein* has two distinct senses:

> Guard and keep safely (in memory)
> and,
> Watch closely to effect destruction.[5]

---

3. The dangerous potential of this text to be read in a misogynistic manner is addressed by Anderson "Feminist Criticism," 103–34.

4. Matthew has also placed the phrase at the center of the pericope.

5. Hayward, *Guarding Head and Heel,* 22, 25–28. See Leg. 3.188–89

Herod, insofar as he is influenced by serpentine dynamics, does the first when he places John in protective custody (Mark 6:17). Herodias embodies the second sense when her hatred of John finally finds its opportunity to have him killed (Mark 6:21). Mark 6:29, describing John's burial, lends some support to this thesis in that the letters in the word for heel, *pterna*, occur in the phrase *ēran to ptōma autou*, they took his corpse.[6]

The narrator complements this portrait by showing Jesus as crucified on the Skull (Mark 15:22), embodying the Hebrew *shūf*, bruise, in Gen 3:15: Her seed will bruise your head.

Even the phenomenon of passing the buck in Gen 3:12, 13 "The woman you gave me . . . the serpent beguiled me" has its physical analogue in the Marcan story in the methodical transfer of John's head from axeman to daughter to mother.[7]

From where does the other non-historical material come? Mark's serpentine folk tradition has a remarkable parallel in Pliny's *Natural History* 10.208:

> Let us ascribe to Phylarchus a marvelous tale about an asp: he relates that in Egypt, when it used to come regularly to be fed at someone's table, it was delivered of young ones, and that its host's son was killed by one of these.

And the gruesome platter that carries the head is not for display to the guests. No such comment is made by the narrator. Rather, it underscores the image of John being devoured as food by the bestial behavior of those around him.[8] The predatory

---

6. If one allows for the interchange of short epsilon and long eta. When Mark 15:45 describes the handing over of Jesus' body to Joseph of Arimathea, he uses the verb edorēsato. Its two nominal forms vacillate between the use of epsilon and eta: dorea and dorēma.

7. And when Jesus has the crowds in the ensuing pericope sit down in garden-plots (*prasiai*, 6:40) Mark is implicitly continuing his narrative interest in the legend of the Garden.

8. For an understanding of this food motif as preparing for Jesus' Eucharist, see Scott, "Dancing Girls," 73n55. The largest collection of texts about various kinds and motivations for beheading is Yarbro-Collins, *Mark*.

dynamic has resonance with the tenor of the Epicurean poetry we find in Lucretius.[9]

One of the subtle contours of the serpentine profile in this narrative is audial. I refer to the preponderance of sibilants in the account of the banquet itself. Allowing for variants in the manuscripts, there are approximately 130 words in the text of Mark 6:14–20. The account of the banquet per se, from 6:21–27a has a similar tally of words. But the number of occurrences of the letter "s" in the first part of the story is approximately 33, while the account of the banquet bears 78 sibilants. Sound slightly suspicious? This banquet is sizzling with more than twice the number of sibilants in the set-up narrative.[10]

II. Of Tongues and Serpents

Prominent in the serpentine profile is the diction-toward-death that we hear from the mouth of the Herodians. And the Marcan narrative bears some similarity to other explorations concerning the deadly tongue in *James* and Lucretius. James 3:7, 8 asserts that all natures, including the reptilian, have been tamed by the human species, but that the tongue remains an untamed source of lethal poison.[11] James, like Mark, is reflecting on the beginning

---

9. *De Rerum Natura*, 5.872–76 describes the fate of species brought to extinction, serving as prey and profit to others. These lines occur in the context of others bearing some resemblance to the proximate setting in Mark. Lines 826–875 describe female forms of life that cease bearing, even as new ones grow up, as well as wool-bearing flocks entrusted to human protection. See Mark 5 and 6 *passim*. Lucretius asserts that the world is comprised of void and indivisible matter (*atomoi*). The very notion of *a-tomos* "that which cannot be further divided" may have attracted the Marcan storyteller to Lucretius in order, in the John pericope, to explore the results of breaking the union of husband and wife. One decision to cut apart leads to another.

10. Friedlander, "Pattern of Sound and Atomistic Theory in Lucretius," 351–370 reveals parallel concerns, in this Epicurean poet, for the link between sound and sense.

11. For parallels, see Laws, *James*, 154; and Burchard, *Jakobusbrief*, 146–48.

of Genesis.[12] This *topos* of the untamed tongue is similar to the Marcan narrative inasmuch as Herodias wanted to kill John but could not, at least until the right opportunity arose to announce his death sentence. This shared theme in Mark and James is complemented by several other aspects of James in Mark 6.[13] And in 6:27, Mark uses the Latin loanword *spekoulator* for John's executioner, perhaps acknowledging some partial truth in the assertion of Lucretius that a random-looking and often-dangerous world is characterized by the proliferation of various tongues.[14]

III. "Brood of Vipers"

Clearly there is some relationship between Q's accusation "brood of vipers" in the preaching of John the Baptist and Mark's serpentine profile swirling around John.[15] It is unclear to me in which direction that influence went. But we can say that the *Life of Adam and Eve* 16:4, 5, like this Marcan narrative, hints at, but

12. McCartney, *James*, 191.

13. James discusses the wisdom from above and avoiding partiality in the synagogue. The letter is addressed to the twelve tribes of the diaspora and discusses healing using oil; celebrates the prophet Elijah, and excoriates the offering of empty good wishes to the poor. Within the pericope about the murder, we find several other parallels to James: warnings against double-mindedness, friendship with the world, oath-taking, adultery and murder, as well as injunctions to be slow to speak and to recall sinners.

14. In *De Rerum Natura*, 5.1028–1090, Lucretius waxes eloquent about the variety of tongues present in the nature of things. Indeed, one might well consider the formative role played at some stage of the storytelling by the interplay between Latin *nex* = murder, violent death and *nexus* = coils of a snake. I judge it a very fruitful avenue for future research to examine the extent of Mark's dialogue with Lucretius. Especially insightful is the treatment of Lucretius by Nussbaum, *The Therapy of Desire*, esp. chs. 5–7, 140–279.

15. Rothschild, *Baptist Traditions*, 156–62 details the heavy distribution of Q parallels in Mark 6–13. Murphy, *John the Baptist*, 132 discusses the saying in the context of purity concerns and the Genesis portrait of the initial state of the serpent as being "blessed with legs." For the Matthean slant on the saying, see Keener "Brood of Vipers."

falls short of, a full identification of the snake with Satan.[16] Mark does so by twice noting that things happened *rapidly* in the narrative of John's murder (Mark 6:25, 27), an echo of the activity of Satan who *immediately* takes away the Word (Mark 4:15).[17]

Conclusion

In this essay, I have highlighted the implicit and lethal partner in the unfolding drama of John's murder. And Mark is not alone in considering serpentine dynamics in the post-Herodian era.[18] But the Evangelist is not interested in reptilian anatomy or history for its own sake. The implicit snake imagery functions as part of a sober tale of warning by the Evangelist concerning some of

16. For text, see Charlesworth, *Pseudepigrapha*, 277.

17. Other aspects of the fate of the seed/word in the execution narrative include "hearing gladly"; falling away in time of persecution (executing John at the behest of others), and being choked by riches and the cares of the world (being personally motivated to execute John at the behest of others). Marcus, *Mark 1–8*, 403 is one among the most thorough commentators who link the events of the pericope with the fate of the seed/Word in Mark 4. And on pages 398–99, he is correct to say that Mark's ascription of the title "king" to Herod is an ironic attestation. It certainly coheres with the way in which Herod's story acts to illustrate the negative aspects of the seed parable of the kingdom in Mark 4.

18. When the apostle Paul, in 2 Cor 11, castigates the Corinthians for being seduced away from their original spouse, he compares the situation to the serpent's cunning seduction of the human couple away from God. In that chapter's last verse, he adds a very interesting and much controverted tagline to an account of his escape from Damascus. Paul refers to his eluding an underling of King Aretas. What is interesting for our immediate purposes is the fact that Aretas was the Nabatean king whose daughter (which one is disputed) was the first wife of Herod Antipas. It was that daughter who was thrown over by Herod in order to take his relative Herodias to wife. I am not suggesting that there is any direct literary dependence of Mark on Paul at this point. Rather, I would suggest that the story of Herod's "divorce" from the Nabatean princess was widely known and that the circumstances and motives involved were the cause of widespread speculation. I have here suggested that one such strain of popular theologizing shows up in the Gospel of Mark, reflecting popular oral culture.

the negative emotional reactions that are provoked by the presence of the Word in the world.[19] Nor is this *monitum* intended to function alone. If the venomous tongue described by James produces results way out of proportion to its size, much more would Mark have his hearers remember that the Word sometimes produces results that are extravagantly, miraculously out of proportion to its initial size. The very next pericope has Jesus feeding 5000. Mark's tale of murder and intrigue is conjoined to and subordinated to his proclamation of the successful advent of the definitive reign of God in Christ.

19. Moloney, "Mark 6:6b–30: Mission, the Baptist, and Failure," also sees this episode as having a didactic purpose for the disciples.

Four

'Ayin and Entrance in Luke 1 and 2

LUKE'S ACCOUNT, BASED ON "eyewitnesses and ministers of the word," displays at least two compositional principles in chapters 1 and 2. First, the Evangelist systematically structures his story with elements of the Greek Chronicler in view. Secondly, he is in dialogue with the Jewish Scriptures as described in Luke 24:44 "Law, Prophets, and Psalms." Each of these has found a voice in commentaries to some degree, and this essay will point out some new detail in those portraits. But the main task of this study is to examine two primary ways in which these structuring principles are specified. That is, I will here explore some of the texture provided the narrative by words beginning with Hebrew 'Ayin. And I will give extended attention to the ways in which Pss. 15–24 have informed Luke 1 and 2. For the sociological background to the process I envision, I take a cue from a recent article by John N. Collins who suggests that *autoptai*/eyewitnesses are those who personally examine the documents available to the community and that *hypēretai*/servants, on the model of Luke 4:20, refer to what could be called the librarians/curators of those same documents. That is, the opening of the Gospel of Luke is profoundly enmeshed in literary dynamics of reading and creative interpretation.[1]

1. Collins "Re-thinking 'Eyewitnesses' in the Light of 'Servants of the Word.'" Like those who do an autopsy, the eyewitnesses examine evidence after those facts have occurred that produced the evidence. In a related vein, I appreciate with Karl Kuhn the parallels between aspects of the infancy narratives and several of the kerygmatic speeches in Acts. However, I do not follow him

I. 1 Chronicles, 2 Chronicles and Lk 1 and 2

Commentators have long seen the special interest taken by the Greek Chronicler in telling the story of Israel in such a way that special attention is given to the role of Jerusalem, its temple and cult. L. T. Brodie has extended that appreciation and drawn readers' attention to the ways in which the Chronicler's work informs the shape of Luke 1–4.[2] I present here part of his summary table describing that interaction.

Preparation for David's reign (1 Chron 1–10)	Preparation for Jesus' Davidic reign (Luke 1:1–25)
Nathan announces David's reign (11–12; 17)	Gabriel announces Jesus' reign (1:26–38)
The ark in the hills (ch. 13)	Mary in the hill-country (1:39–45, 56)
God gives David victory (14; 18–20)	Mary's victorious Magnificat (1:46–55)
Priestly service, sons and song (15–16)	Zechariah, his son and his song (1:57–80)
The census & origin of the Temple (21–22)	The census and the birth of Jesus (2:1–20)
The people and piety of the Temple (23–29)	People and piety around Jesus (2:21–38)
The building of the Temple (2 Chron 1:1—5:1)	Jesus grows up (2:39–40)

in his inference that the characters of Luke 1 and 2 were among the witnesses who helped shape the traditions embodied in those speeches. See Kuhn "Beginning the Witness," esp. 251. And while I agree with Raymond Brown that these chapters combine some history with theological reflection, it is not my intent here to isolate the historical kernels as such, much less opine about the subsequent role of the principals. See Brown *Birth of the Messiah*, 697-712. My chief interest here resides in that history constituted by Luke's interaction with the texts specified.

2. Brodie, "A New Temple and a New Law," 24; also see Endres, "The Spiritual Vision of Chronicles."

The Lord takes possession of the Temple (5:2—9:1)	Jesus in the Temple (2:41–52)
Life and decline of the Temple (chs. 10–36)	

In his more detailed studies of these parallels, Brodie provides data helpful in understanding some of the more puzzling aspects of the text. For example, he correlates the punishment of Saul for not believing the word (1 Chron 10:13–14) with what he calls a punishment of Zechariah for a similar offense in Luke 1:20.[3]

Within this agenda set by his dialogue with the Chronicler, two other more recent phenomena help to shape the infancy narrative: some of the literary remains of the Pauline mission, as well as the destruction of Jerusalem in CE 70. There is sufficient overlap between the themes of Galatians and the infancy narrative to suggest that it is a conversation partner in Luke's formulation.[4] And I join others in suggesting that the Evangelist has a particular concern to address the issue of Jerusalem's Second Temple having been destroyed by Roman forces. Luke wants to address concerns about God's fidelity, given the tragedy of CE 70. I would suggest that he does so in part by exegeting the name Jerusalem in Luke 1 and 2. The component parts of the name Jerusalem in popular etymology refer to *holy* and *peace*. Within Luke 1 and 2, the preponderance of occurrences of *hagios*, holy, reside in Luke 1. And within chapters 1 and 2 the majority of the occurrences of *eirēnē*, peace, are in Luke 2 (with one occurrence at the border of the two chapters, in 1:79). Luke is suggesting that, while the city has been destroyed by the time of his writing, the promises of God's holy presence and peace have not failed Israel.

---

3. Brodie, "A New Temple and a New Law," 27.

4. Shared themes include attention to the Law, angels, sent from God, children of promise, born of woman, circumcision, Jerusalem. And perhaps most dramatically present in both is the pain and anxiety attendant on the formation of Christ (cp. Gal 4:19 ōdinō and Lk 2:48 ōdynesthai).

II. *'Ayin* **and Luke 1 and 2**

In addition, Luke's transformation of Chronicles is remotely specified by Hebrew words with initial *'Ayin*. *'Ayin*, while the name of a letter, is also the word for *eye*. Thus, it provides a ready vehicle for amplifying an account of "eyewitnesses and ministers of the word." Consensus holds that the Evangelist in chapters 1 and 2 is not translating a Hebrew narrative into Greek.[5] And I agree. What I am suggesting is something slightly different. I think that the following data suggest an author (aided by an authorial community) who, while writing the infancy narrative in Greek, draws on a portion of the Hebrew lexicon for some of the thematic contours of his presentation. Elsewhere, Luke has paid careful attention to publicly observable data concerning the ministry of the adult Jesus. In the infancy narratives, he is engaged in a particular kind of bilingual theological endeavor that anticipates part of Jesus' ministry.

Listed here in the proximate order of their occurrence in the Hebrew lexicon are instances of words beginning with *'ayin*, with citation of at least one occurrence of a Greek equivalent in Luke 1 and 2. Perhaps the most noteworthy is *'almāh*, young woman of marriageable age (See Luke 1:27.) But there are approximately three dozen more.

Luke

'ebed	Servant 1:48; 2:29
'ad	Perpetuity 1:33
'ēder	Flock 2:8
'uwd	Return 1:56; 2:45
'āwōn	Iniquity 1:77
'ăwîyl	Young boy 1:80; 2:43

5. Jung, *The Original Language of the Lukan Infancy Narrative*; The issue of Semitisms is named a "difficult" one by Bovon, *Luke 1: A Commentary*, 4.

31

'āṭāh	Wrap 2:7
'āzab	Set free 1:68
'ōz	Strength 1:51
'ayin	Eye 1:2; 2:30
'ākar	Trouble 1:29
'ālāh	Ascend 2:4, 42
'Elyōwn	Most High 1:76; 2:14
'ōwlēl	Child 2:16
'ālas	Rejoice 1:44, 47
'ālats	Exult, jump for joy 1:44, 47
ma'ămād	Office 1:8
'am	People 1:10, 21; 2:32; Kinsman 1:36, 2:44
'im	With 1:28
'ānāh	Answer, respond 1:19, 35
'ōnāh	Cohabit 2:36
'ānāh	Be occupied with 2:37
'ēth	Time 1:57; 2:6
'ānāwim	Poor, humble 1:52
'ātsab	Hurt, pain, grieve 2:48
'ātsuwm	Numerous 2:13
'ătsārāh	Assembly 2:13
'arēl	(Uncircumcised) 1:20
'āriyts	Awe-inspiring, terror-striking 1:65; 2:9
'ăriyriy	Childless 1:7
'āšiyr	Rich 1:53
'āthiyd	Prepared 2:31
'āthēq	Advance (in years) 2:36
'āthar	Pray 2:37.

Luke or his source's use of Hebrew *'Ayin* is reflected in the behavior of Anna. One of the meanings of *'Ānāh*, beginning with *'Ayin*, is "be occupied with". This concept is part of the portrait of Anna and her continual Temple services of fasting and prayer in Luke 2:37. The rhyme of the letter *'ayin* with *zayin* is also helpful in understanding Luke's procedure. *Zayin* constitutes a soft rhyme with *Tsiōn*, the site of the divine presence as experienced in the temple, where some of the events of Luke 1 and 2 transpire. And *Zayin* is the 7th letter in the alphabet. The seventh position of zayin, I would suggest, is one of the reasons for associating the number 7 with Anna in Luke 2:36. And her age, presented as 84, is I think, directing us to Psalm 84, which begins "How lovely is your dwelling place, O Lord of hosts."

III. Law, Prophets and Psalms

These, say the mysterious stranger in Luke 24:44, reveal who he is. In Luke 1 and 2, the Evangelist renders a version of all three.

Law

Nomos occurs 5 times (2:22 ,23, 24, 27, 39). The equivalents for the five books of Moses are:

- Genesis—creation

    Emphasis on matter and word (Elizabeth and Zechariah and God)

    Emphasis on *hrēma*, word, along the lines of Hebrews 11:3 (Mary).[6]

    Surprising birth to Abram and Sara.[7]

---

6. These two approaches to the mode of the divine creative act may be related to the two ways in which the opening Hebrew phrase of Gen 1:1 may be read.

7. Green, "The Problem of a Beginning," 68–78.

- Exodus—"deliver"
- Leviticus—Temple cult
- Numbers—census
- Deuteronomy—farewell of Simeon

Prophets

- Prior to the 3 Major Prophets: The one born from the house of Elisha (Eliza-beth) goes forth in the spirit of Elijah 1:17.

- Isaiah—Four Servant songs formally reflected in the 4 "songs" of Lk 1 and 2: Magnificat, Benedictus, Gloria, Nunc Dimittis.

- Plus the content of the Servant Songs are spread throughout Lk 1 and 2:

Isaiah		*Luke's four "songs"*
49:1	called from the womb	1:15, 31
49:1	named my name	1:13, 31; 2:21
49:2	like a sharp sword in shadow of his hand	2:35
49:5	honored in the Lord's eyes	1:48
52:14	highest-glory-wonder	2:14, 18
53:1	to whom has the arm of Lord been revealed?	2:28

- Jeremiah 4:4 circumcise yourselves, remove the foreskin of your hearts
- Ezekiel—return to Jerusalem
- The Book of the Twelve prophets—Jesus at twelve discussing the Law

Psalms

Psalms 15 and 24 are psalms that may have functioned as entrance liturgies at the Temple in Jerusalem. So argues Patrick Miller.[8] I want to explore the ways in which these Psalms have themselves been mined, and bracket other Psalms that seem to have been mined, by Luke in the creation of the narratives in Luke 1 and 2. The birth and childhood narratives both begin and end in Jerusalem, as do Psalms 15 and 24. And the questioning that characterizes the beginning and end of Luke 1 and 2 is also present in Psalms 15 and 24.

The symmetry of these Psalms runs thus:

Pss.		Pss.
15	entrance liturgy	24
16	trust	23
17	petition for help	22
18	royal	20, 21
19	Law	

In this setting, the Law is central. And the God of Luke 1 and 2 is one who would be known in Law: The word *theos* occurs 19 times in Luke 1 and 2.

Listed here in order of the appearance in Luke of these Psalmic parallels:

Luke 1		Psalms
	Zechariah	
1:9	Mountain of Lord	15, 24
1:21	Sojourn in your tent	15

---

8. Miller, "Kingship, Torah Obedience, and Prayer,"

Gospel Essays

	Gabriel	
1:30–33	David-grace-forever	18
	Elizabeth	
1:45	Promise of the Lord proves true	18
	Mary	
1:46, 47	Exalted God of my salvation	18
1:49	Praises to your Name	18
1:53	The poor shall eat and be satisfied	22
1:47, 48	You will save a humble people, / and humble proud eyes	18
	Zechariah	
1:68	I bless the Lord who counsels me	16
1:71	Those who hated me	18
1:69	Horn of salvation	18
1:71	Savior of those who seek refuge from / their adversaries at your right hand	17
1:78	The sun comes forth like a champion and joyfully runs its course.	19
Luke 2		Psalms
	Birth of Jesus	
2:11	Lord-save-Christ	20
2:13	Heavens declare the glory of God	19
2:19	Meditation of my heart	19

	Simeon	
2:25	Saints	16
2:30, 31	Satisfied when I behold your face	17
2:30–32	Glory in salvation	21
2:35	Sword—(sign) (via Luke 11:27, 28)	17
2:34	They fell, we rose	20
	Anna	
2:36, 37	Dwell in house of Lord for years to come	23
2:38	Tell of the Lord to the coming generation, proclaiming his deliverance	22

Particularly interesting in the following cluster is the dialogue between Psalm 19 and the continuing portrait of Mary:

	Mary & Joseph	
2:39	All accomplished according to the Law	19, 22
2:46	Life forever (after three days)	21
2:44, 45	Seek the face of the God of Jacob	24
2:49	Ever since my mother bore me you have been my God	22
2:51	Meditation of my heart	19

Note the bifocal objects of meditation in Psalm 19, the heavens' refraction of God's glory, and the Law. At the two analogous points in Luke, Mary *keeps all these things in her heart.* Mary contemplates:

a) at the birth of Jesus, the eruption of heaven's angelic praise of the glory of God and

b) Jesus' discourse with the teachers (of the Law).

IV. Penuel and Asher

Two designators of Anna, Penuel and Asher in Luke 2:36, are important in establishing the unity of these first two chapters as well as one aspect of the Gospel's unity. And it is the notion of "circle" that links Luke's exploration of the two terms.[9]

Concerning Penuel, appearing as Phenuel in Luke 2:36

The name means "face of God." In Ps. 24:6 we read, and I follow the exact word order:

> *This,*
> *the generation of those who seek him out, of those inquiring*
> *after your face,*
>
> *Jacob*

The sense may be rendered "this is Jacob, the generation of those who seek him out, of those inquiring after your face" (*Lord*-implied). But the word order in this case is quite important. By splitting up the phrase "this Jacob" into the beginning and end of the phrase, the Psalmist has created a circle around the rest of the verse. More importantly, the Psalmist thereby casts a circular net around the whole collection of Psalms 15–24, suggesting that the attitudes and actions of the people described in these Psalms together constitute the generation of those who seek the face of the God of Israel. Luke has several people including Anna seek the face of God in various ways in these first two chapters.[10]

9. Luke 2:29 has a similar ring construction: Now *dismiss your servant,* master, / according to your word, / *in peace.*

10. And the entrance liturgy so constructed coheres with Luke's incorporation of the Tamid service here in chapter 1 and at the cross of Jesus in chapter

But the Evangelist also embodies the alternate reading of the verse: "this is the generation of those who seek your face, Jacob," by having Mary look for and inquire of the young Jesus. Jesus, who embodies the Psalmic Torah piety of king and people, *is* Jacob/Israel for Luke.

Concerning Asher

The word opens Psalm 32:1 (Ps. 31 LXX) and means "blessed." It is applied to those whose lawlessness is forgiven. Its tenth verse says "mercy encircles the one who hopes in the Lord." I would suggest that the explicitly named and fallen hopes of the travelers to Emmaus in Luke 24:21 and the things happening in and around Jesus in Luke 24:19 embody Psalm 32:10. They adjoin a circle that connects the Gospel's opening emphasis on forgiveness of sin (Luke 1:77) with the dialogue of the risen Christ about forgiveness of sin (Luke 24:47).

Conclusion

This essay has shown some of the specifics by which Luke does two things in his introduction to the Gospel. The Evangelist situates the Jesus event within Israel's Greek and Hebrew heritage. And the dual reading of Ps. 24:6 in the infancy narrative indicates that "seeking God's face" is to be seen in tandem with "seeking Jesus."

---

23. Hamm, "The Tamid Service in Luke-Acts."

Five

The Latinity of Johannine Witness

JOHN 19:20 TELLS US that the *titulus* on the cross of Jesus was written in Hebrew, Latin, and Greek. It is my contention in this essay that, in addition to the long-recognized traits of Semitic influence on the language of the text, there is a discernible influence of the Latin language. And I would suggest that we wear our Latinate lenses when we read, not just the cross, but many other parts of the text, because some aspects of John find their most aesthetically pleasing explanation in a Latin underpinning. This is not quite the same as identifying an early Latin source of a Greek text as has been done successfully, for example, in studies of Plutarch. For example, the life of Cicero in Plutarch's *Lives* is seen as dependent on the lost Latin text of Suetonius' *Life of Cicero.*[1] Rather, I refer to John's use of widely known lexical and grammatical traits of Latin as part of his agenda to present Jesus as the Word-become-flesh. In part, Jesus is available as a Latin Word through John.

For example, uniquely among the canonical Gospels, John describes the mother of Jesus without any further qualifiers. Her admonition to the servants in 2:5 "Do whatever he tells you" is, I would suggest, directly related to the issue of her title as well as this wedding background. That is, in having her give a mother's advice, *matri-moneo*, the Evangelist has provided a reciprocal interpretive partner to the *matrimonium* that she witnesses. This is at one stroke both elegant and sly.

1. Glucker, "Cicero's Philosophical Associations," 55.

In what follows, we first examine the Latinate aspects of John's Greek before suggesting a possible venue, the Greco-Roman bilingual schools, from which this dynamic may have been generated. I explore traces of such Latin dynamics without making impossible claims to knowledge of the Evangelist's personal background and rather suggest that the self-evident Latinity in places arose in the process of the pre-textual oral formation in catechesis and homiletics. In the final part of this study, we look at some ways in which Johannine spirituality in a Latinate register might be exercised.

I. JOHN'S LATINITY

Our examples of the Greek-Latin interplay approximate the order of their occurrence in the text.

1.1 Horace and John

The opening of the *Ars Poetica* warns against constructing a text that begins with a lovely woman but ends with an ugly fish. (See the mother of Jesus in ch.2 and the catch of fish in ch. 21). And the poet similarly tries to guard the artist against that lamentable moment when s/he asks: That was a wine-jar when the process began, why does it turn out to be a pitcher? (See the wine jars of ch. 2 and the Samaritan Woman's pitcher in ch. 4).

1.2 Horace and John 4

Indeed, Horace's *Ars Poetica* , written to a father-and-son pair, offers parallels that are particularly instructive for understanding chapter four's two proverbs as well as some of the sweep of imagery affecting John 4. In the opening lines 1–23, Horace suggests that in a work marked by noble beginnings, there is a place for one or two glittering *purple passages* to be added. So too John

41

4:35, 37 cites two sayings supposedly known at the time though, as in the case with Horace, we have no independent attestation thereof. One of the examples of such a passage cited by Horace even discusses flowing water and fields, as does the backdrop of the sayings in John 4.

In addition, the fifth declension of nouns in Latin is comprised almost entirely of feminine words, with the exception of *meridianus,* midday, and *dies,* day, which are masculine. This grammatical profile is congruent with the cultural oddity of the Samaritan Woman in ch. 4 being alone at the well at midday, in conversation with a man.[2] More importantly, perhaps, the fifth declension was comprised of nouns of heterogeneous ancestry, the literary equivalent of the mixed-race composition of the Samaritans.[3] It would be naïve, I think, to overlook John's conscious dialogue with Horace, or the shared worldview of both writers that recognizes in their literary products a mixture of fact and artifice.

1.3 Varronian Latin Grammar in John 4[4]

Varro (first century BCE) attempted a comprehensive study of the Latin language. Varro (*De Lingua Latina,* 8.5) cites *impositio,* imposition of a name, as one source of words, and images that process as a spring. See John 4:26's I AM in context of the spring welling up in believers.

Varro (*LL,* 10.44) discusses the *ratio,* relationship, between the genders of given word forms and the cases into which they are declined. The example he uses is the nominative, genitive, and dative, as well as the masculine, feminine, and neuter forms of *albus,* white. See the description in John 4:35 of the white fields in context of the single woman and plural disciples (4:27,28).

---

2. Neyrey, "What's Wrong with This Picture?"
3. Sihler, *A New Comparative Grammar,* 341.
4. Taylor, *Declinatio,* 26, 47, 81.

Varro (*LL*, 10.15) when discussing words that can be changed in their form, says that some words are derived by will, *voluntas*. This happens when anyone whatsoever imposes a name from some thing onto another thing. And derivational morphology, says Varro, involving changes of case, gender and number, reflects people's linguistic usage (*consuetudo*). Consider in this context Jesus' declaring in 4:34 that his food is to do the *will* of the One who sent him and the Samaritan woman's assertion in 4:9 that Jews have nothing to do with, (literally) *do not have common usage with* Samaritans.

1.4 Latin Lexical Order in John 4

In Mark 6, the Evangelist has juxtaposed narratives about a storm and a feeding. The Hebrew analogues for those phenomena are items proximate to each other in the lexicon: *sa 'ah*/storm and *sapha'* /feed. The Fourth Evangelist has carried on and greatly expanded this procedure throughout John: This chapter is rife with clusters of words that are near each other in Latin. These clusters, within a few pages of each other in the respective lexica, are spread throughout this fourth chapter of John. Of course, there is no surety about the precise shape of ancient lexica in any given period and many words frequently have more than one referent or nuance attached to them.[5] But bearing that in mind, what follows is a list of plausible analogues in Latin for the Greek diction of this chapter.

Latin

- lassus: weary, tired.
- latex: running water, stream
- urbs: city
- urna: water-pitcher

5. Green, *Chasing the Sun*, ch. 1.

Gospel Essays

- divus: pertaining to a god
- doceo: teach
- domus: house
- donum: gift
- duco: draw
- salarium: pay, wages
- salus: safety, welfare, salvation
- Samaria
- miror: wonder at
- mitto: send
- mons: mountain
- fatigo: be weary, tired
- fatiloquus: prophet
- febris: fever
- femina: woman
- fessus: tired
- festus: festival
- fido: believe in
- filius: son
- fons: a spring, flow of water
- voluntas: will
- vivo: live
- vulgo: communicate,make accessible to all
- opus: work
- orbis: world
- orior: welling up
- ostento: make known

- orca: earthenware jar with a large belly
- orno: provide with necessaries
- Horae: The Hours; goddesses presiding over the change of seasons
- homo: person
- honor: honor
- hora: hour
- hospitalitas: hospitality
- humilis: low
- Hymen: god of marriage
- meridianus: midday
- meto: gather harvest
- aggredior: approach a person
- agnosco: perceive
- agrestis: pertaining to a field
- aio . . . ais-ne: is it possible?
- albus: white
- alibi: here . . . there
- alimentum: food
- alius: other
- bibo: give to drink
- biduum: two days
- bes: two-thirds of anything comprised of 12 items; containing the number 8. ("h" is the eighth letter; see 4:1–2; several rough breathings and a nine-word aside).
- tener: young
- terra: earth, world
- testor: bear witness

- coram: personally, oneself
- convocatio: a calling together
- converto: direct one's attention or look towards
- credo: believe
- convalesco: recover
- convivium: feast

1.5 The Lacuna in John 4–6

In John 4, Jesus journeys from Samaria to Galilee. In John 5, he is suddenly in Jerusalem, with no explanation offered by the narrator as to how he got there. In John 6, the text situates him in Galilee. Is there a geographical *lacuna* between chapters 4 and 6? Yes there is. It's called the Pool of Bethesda, and it's sitting in verses 1–9. *Lacuna* = lake.

1.6 Principium John 8:25

The question of 8:25a "Who are you?" is answered with the phrase *tēn archēn o ti kai lalō hymin.* It is possible to recognize in the expression *tēn archēn* a Latin neuter subject whose form in the nominative is identical to that in the accusative. Then we hear the Latinate voice of Jesus say "The *principium.*" One might then read the o ti as a quotation mark that in this case precedes the question "And do I continue to speak to you?" The principium may be seen in its philosophical sense of generating-first-principle, or in the republican political sense of first-voter chosen to lead by example on a given piece of proposed legislation.

1.7 The Good and the True

In ancient philosophy, the transcendentals, beauty, goodness, truth, were perceived to be convertible, because of their essential unity. So it comes as no surprise to hear that Jesus the Good Shepherd is contrasted with the false shepherds in John 10. The Evangelist is exploring *bonum* and *verum*. But it is even more interesting, perhaps, that one of the established meanings of *bonus* is "surplus." And so we hear the Jesus of chapter 10 insist that he has come not just to give life, but to give it abundantly.

1.8a AUCTORITAS-VERITAS

The Latin behind *exousia* in 1:12 is AUCTORITAS. Its component parts are developed in ch. 5:

> Actor/Auctor: The Son does only what he sees the Father doing.
>
> Auctoritas: And he (the Father) gave him authority to effect judgment.

The Latin behind *alētheia* in 1:17 is VERITAS. It is articulated in a Latin hologram in 14:6. I am the way (via), the truth (veritas) and the life (vita). And the Greek equivalents of both AUCTORITAS and VERITAS occur in proximity to each other again in John 17:2, 17. The initial letters of both words, A and V, span the original Latin alphabet and are in that regard comprehensive. With some simplification, I use "original" here to refer to that derived from Etruscan. And it may be the case that John has used these words as templates to guide his descriptions of Father-Spirit-Son.

Father : *Auctor-Vita* "Just as the Father raises from the dead and gives life" (5:21). "Just as the Father has Life in himself . . ." (5:26).

Son: *Actor- Veritas* "I have completed the work you have given me to do . . . (17:4). I gave them your word (17:14) Your word is truth (17:17).

Spirit: *Via-Auctoritas* "The wind blows and you hear its sound but you do not know whence it comes or where it is going" (3:8); "The Father gave him authority to effect judgment; just as I hear, I judge" (5:27, 30).

1.8b Relations among parts of AUCTORITAS-VERITAS

When one thinks with the Evangelist in terms of these three descriptive phrases, the next obvious question becomes "What do we make of the terms that "remain over" in the relation of one word to another?" For example, concerning AUCTOR-ACTOR, what remains over is U. Concerning VITA and VIA, what remains over is T. Together they comprise UT, the purpose particle "in order that." If indeed this Latinate agenda is present in the text, one might expect there to be a subsidiary trace of UT. That is exactly what we have in the 145 occurrences of *hina*, in order that. This is approximately triple the number of its occurrences in any of the Synoptic Gospels.

Concerning VERITAS and VITA, what remains over is RES. This broad-ranging term can mean "lawsuit," and that has long been recognized in the diction of the Gospel, especially in chapters 5–10. RES also means "dowry." Out of deference to the memory of the historical Jesus that asserts his unmarried status, we should not expect this to be clearly represented. And there has been some reticence of late to see betrothal imagery in places such as John 4.[6] But a close approximation to dowry issues may be implied in the discussion of the bridegroom in chapter 3. This is especially so in 3:35 "The Father loves the Son and has put everything into his hand" when seen together with Jesus' handing over the Spirit as he gives the two at the foot of his cross to one another.

---

6. Arterbury, "Breaking the Betrothal Bonds."

1.8c AUCTORITAS-VERITAS
and the Resurrection saying

In John 11:25, we hear Jesus say, "I am the resurrection and the life." Our previous reflection on AUCTORITAS-VERITAS suggests, in a fascinating way, a possible genesis for that saying. Here are the three phrases, this time with the letters needed to spell *resurrectio* in bold print.

a**UC**t**O**r vita

actor v**ERITAS**

via auctoritas

That the Evangelist or a community prophet generated the combination of *resurrectio* and *vita,* resurrection and life, from this amalgam is made even more likely in that *resurrectio* fits perfectly from a numerological point of view between the first and second lines. That is, what we have are three phrases that successively contain 10, 12, and 13 letters. The fuller paradigm looks like this:

a**UC**t**O**r vita

RESURRECTIO

actor v**ERITAS**

via auctoritas

And this is no idle word game. Whereas in the Pauline and Synoptic corpora, reflection on Jesus' resurrection in the light of Scripture reveals the truth of his claim to a distinctive relationship with Father and Spirit, the situation is different in this part of John. In John 20:8, the Beloved Disciple's belief at the empty tomb is explicitly dissociated from any reflection on *Scriptures* about resurrection.[7] I would suggest that the complex we have

---

7. O'Brien, "Written That You May Believe."

just examined may be one of the causes in narrative time that generate the faith of the Beloved Disciple in chapter 20.

1.9 Ab-lat

Only in John do we read that water and blood were then drawn *from his side* (19:34). In the Latin, this would involve *ab* and the word *latus*. *Ab-lat-ive* of course is the last of the cases in Latin declension, and one not used in Greek. The advantage of this grammatical reading of the crucifixion resides in recognizing the Word's full declension in the flesh of our condition.

1.10 Synoptic Centurion Transformed in the Pisteuein (100x) of John

One of the puzzling aspects of Mark's Gospel is that there is a narrative analogue for each kind of seed described in Mark 4, with the exception of the abundant, hundredfold harvest. I would suggest that the role of a centurion as (at least theoretically) a leader of 100 soldiers has some bearing on this issue. In the Marcan *centurion*'s confession at the cross of Jesus, the hundredfold harvest of faith is at least formally suggested. While John has no scene involving a literal Roman centurion, the 100 value of the *centurion*'s faith is represented by the 100 Johannine occurrences of the verb *pisteuein*, to believe.

1.11 Peter and the Beloved Disciple in ch. 20: Gerund and Direct Object.

One of the most elegant and I think, potent samples of disciples-as-words being expressed with and in Jesus occurs in chapter 20, in the race to the empty tomb. In 20:1–10, the tomb becomes the terminus of a theological sentence, and the activity of running provides the context in which one may examine Peter under the grammatical rubric of gerund and the Beloved Disciple under that of direct object.

Gerund, from a root meaning among other things to *hold public office,* is a verbal noun. "Running" itself is a good example of a gerund. One construction involving the gerund and a direct object stipulates that the gerund exhibit the case required by the verb and that the object follow the composite verb and gerund, as in this example:

> Discimus legendo libros.
> We learn by reading books.

However, in practice, Latin speakers preferred that the object be removed from the end of the sentence to a place before the gerund. The object then exhibits the case in which the gerund would appear and the former gerund becomes a gerundive, a verbal adjective, which agrees with the former direct object noun, as in this transformed example:

> Discimus libris legendis
> We learn by books-reading.

Both constructions mean the same, but in the latter, the status of the object is shifted in relation to the gerund.

In ch. 20, Peter functions as a gerund and the Disciple whom Jesus loves as the direct object. Indeed, the very appellation of *the one whom Jesus loves* serves first and foremost to embody the idea of a direct object. That disciple, though arriving at the terminus first, lets Peter go ahead to that position. In the process, a) the disciple whom Jesus loves acquires the case-status of primary subject of the action exhibited by Peter (cf. 20:2, 3 with 20:5, 6), and b) Peter's seeing is not primary but merely "agrees with" the other disciple's antecedent action (20:5, 6).[8] Peter, who might have been the believing subject of this coming-to-believe narrative has become a modifier to the believing-narrative of the disciple whom Jesus loves (20:8).

---

8. Wheelock, *Latin,* 188.

II. POSSIBLE SOCIAL BACKGROUND: THE GRECO-ROMAN SCHOOLS

Latin was of course disseminated throughout the republic and Empire in non-scholastic venues.[9] But at the end of the first century, Quintilian was promoting a program in the schools in which Greek and Latin were on an equal footing. Study of the schools in which this happened continues to grow at a steady pace.[10]

Through the optics of these studies, we may recognize afresh just how deeply John's project would be recognizable to those who had taken part in the school system or had heard about its characteristics by other means. The following "classroom" aspects of GJn, while not the primary referents of the text, function to give the Gospel a profile also related to the experience of learning. Consideration of the dynamics we have examined in Part One are more important than possible generating matrices. But if only 60 percent of these historical suggestions are plausible, that would justify further consideration of the role of the bilingual schools on the oral tradents of the Johannine formulae. For example:

- The *pedagogue* led the child to the teacher. See Andrew who does the same for Simon, *bringing* him to Jesus in John 1; Andrew next appears with the *paidarion* in John 6.

- Jesus is explicitly "teacher" in 1:38; 3:10.

- After every eight days, there was a suspension of teaching called *nundinae*, market days. See John 1:29, 35, 43; 2:1, 12.

- The teacher's whip, *scutica*, was a frequent part of depictions of the classroom, in art and literature. See John 2:15.

- MN and *athbash*. One of the exercises at the elementary level involved learning the Greek alphabet by reciting its first

9. Ostler, *Ad Infinitum*, 49–53.

10. Marrou, *History of Education*; Bonner, *Education in Ancient Rome*; Cribiore, *Gymnastics of the Mind*; Joyal, *Greek and Roman Education*.

and last letters together and moving progressively toward the middle of the alphabet in recitation. That center resides in MN. Should we hear in John's characteristic expression *Amen Amen* an echo of the center that holds together two directions in itself? Should we hear *Amen Amen* in part as the comprehensive voice of the One in whom all linguistic expression finds its coherence?

• Grammar and rhetoric lessons were often separated by a noontime bath and lunch. See John 4–6.

• The educator often helped with the tasks of feeding the infants; should we see Jesus the educator/nutritionist in John 6?

• The expulsion of a black sheep among students was sometimes necessary: Varro tells us "Often a single wanton and dirty boy defiles the flock". Judas in John 13 is described as both *not clean* and as a *thief*.[11]

• The verb *klinō* that the Evangelist employs to say that Jesus "inclined his head" in John 19:30 is also the verb used to refer to the recitation of a noun in different cases.

III. JOHANNINE SPIRITUALITY in LATINATE REGISTER

Appropriation of Johannine Latinity in contemporary spirituality will be examined here in three regards: virtue, ecumenism, and Eucharist.

Virtue

We have already suggested above that John appropriates the language of Auctoritas-Veritas to describe the work of Father, Son, and Spirit. Again, John's equations seem to be:

11. Muller, *Varros*, 52, 53; Wright, "Greco-Roman Character Typing"; Bonner, *Education in Ancient Rome*, 142, 134.

Father - AUCTOR VITA
Spirit- VIA AUCTORITAS
Son- ACTOR VERITAS

This paradigm is useful both for further elucidating the Persons themselves as well as for exploring the faith and love that they evoke.

Of course, there is no explicit formulation using the term "Trinity" in John. That is a late second-century term. But a long-standing theological tradition, owing much to Augustine and Aquinas, holds that God's knowing and loving God's self constitute the very Persons of the Trinity. And John anticipates some aspects of what will eventually be explored as the doctrine of the blessed Trinity. Admittedly with the advantage of hindsight, we may see that John's phrase VIA AUCTORITAS refers to the Spirit. In its VIA we may see the mutual bestowal of love between Father and Son. In its AUCTORITAS, we may see the breathing forth of the very Person of uncreated Love.[12] And in John's ACTOR VERITAS, we may see an anticipation of the teaching about the Son as perfect, full, and true expression of the Father's identity.

We also have in John 4: 23, 24 what appears to be a reflection related to AUCTORITAS-VERITAS in the exhortation to "worship the Father in Spirit and Truth." In what follows, I trace the ways in which the Johannine language of love and believing/knowing is integrated into that agenda.

Father: In 4:43–54, we have the paronomastic presentation of the Father/father identified in the giving of life. (Father: *Auctor Vitae*).

Spirit: In 4:29, 39 we have a reflection on love's way, corresponding to the Spirit, the *Via-Auctoritas*. The Samaritan woman declares in 4:29, 39 that she has met someone who "told me everything I've done". This is an obvious exaggeration; it is hyperbole. And that is what makes it a fitting extrapolation from the vision of love's excellent way (*kath hyperbolēn hodon*) in 1 Cor

12. Torrell, *St. Thomas*, 184–85.

12:31 and the ensuing chapter 13 in which Paul asserts that "If I speak in the tongues of men . . . but have not love, I am nothing."

Son: In both 4:23, 24 there is a double pattern that may be seen as related to the Son, the *Actor Veritas* of John's agenda. In both verses we have:

> 23 & 24
>
> Worship
> Spirit & Truth
> Worship

This double repetition of *truth* may be considered as analogous to the frequent and distinctively Johannine expression *Amen Amen* that affirms something as true, and here constitutes the Truth/Son's witness to Father (vs. 23) and Spirit (vs. 24). The witness to Spirit in verse 24 is to God as Spirit, inclusive of the One who will later in the text appear as the Paraclete and who will in subsequent church history be identified as the person of the Holy Spirit.

The ideational affirmations concerning truth here are complemented by a proliferation of verbs having to do with believing and knowing. Jesus' appeal in 4:21 to "Believe me, woman" is part of a pattern of 7 occurrences of *believe* in this chapter (4:21,39,41,42,48,50,53) and 8 of verbs to know (*oida* 4:10,22,22,25,32,42; *ginōskō* 4:1,53).

The reciprocal loving and knowing at the center of the Trinity's action, partly anticipated by the implicit loving and explicit knowing in John 4, is made available in the knowing/believing and loving of the church. To that church we now turn.

Ecumenism

The distinctive Latinate anticipation in John of reflections on the Trinity may perhaps best be seen in its practical dimensions in relation to the call of Walter Kasper for Christians to engage in a spiritual ecumenism of life, love, and truth. By this he refers to shared study and prayer, as well as events of joint witness and service to the world.[13] The Latinate underpinnings of John's reflection on Father, Son, and Spirit in the Fourth Gospel make a contribution to ecumenical study in that the Evangelist addresses one of the ongoing points of contention between Orthodox and other Christian believers.

The AUCTORITAS-VERITAS construction offers a supple treasure of reflection useful in mediating the divergent emphases of Eastern and Latin Christianity concerning the tri-personal God. The East has traditionally insisted that the Father alone sends both Son and Spirit, an assertion that safeguards one sense of the Father's monarchy and the distinctness of Son and Spirit. That is well supported in John when one views the A-V construction with special attention to the ITAS ending shared only by the Son and Spirit. Additionally, AUCTOR VITA holds a distinctive status, more evenly proportioned, as compared with the relatively lopsided constructions of VIA AUCTORITAS and ACTOR VERITAS when their respective sense phrases are spelled out:

AUCTOR VITAE.
VIA AUCTORITATIS
ACTOR VERITATIS

Concomitantly, the Western church has not been shy in focusing on the mutual breathing forth of the Spirit by both Father and Son. That too is amply documented in the A-V construction when one concentrates on the similar ordering of the Father and Son from A to V, AUCTOR VITA and ACTOR VERITAS, with the quite different ordering of the Spirit from V to A, VIA AUCTORITAS. One should also note in this context the aspiration needed to articulate the initial V of the phrase VIA AUCTORITAS.

13. Kasper, *That They May All be One*, 72–73.

Eucharist

The kind and quality of Latinate dynamics in John suggest, I think, a thoroughgoing Eucharistic profile to the text. Latin has been incorporated into the final Greek text in such a way that while present in the new medium of Greek, its peculiar stylistic and lexical traits have often been preserved. The larger theological horizon would seem to suggest that this process is analogous to what is happening in John's Eucharistic community where incorporation and transformation are the rule. The suspicion of this Eucharistic horizon is only further confirmed when we remember that Jesus never prays privately in John; that he is both communication from the Father and response thereto (14:7; 11:42). This converse into which the disciples are drawn is thoroughly liturgical.

Conclusion

This formal investigation of the Latinity of the Fourth Gospel opens a window onto a worldview that may have been partly nurtured in the schools per se and conversant with that world's languages on their own terms. The Latin of John's world not only assists us in a more textured and satisfying understanding of that Gospel, but the Latinity of John's witness bears the potential to inform the church's most basic reflections about its identity in relation to the tri-personal God.

six

John 20: Jesus Christ
in Johannine Concert

COMMENTATORS HAVE LONG NOTED that there are echoes of the
Song of Songs in the encounter between Jesus and Mary Magdalene. The burden of this essay is to suggest that we listen more
carefully to the music of John's theology in John 20. I suggest that
John 20 presents Jesus Christ "in concert," that is, as both head
and members acting partly under the influence of musicological
dynamics. The author of the Gospel does so by drawing an inter-
textual portrait relying on resources in both the Pauline corpus
and the Psalms. And I assume that this intertextuality is a result
of previous homiletic and catechetical exploration that occurred
in John's eucharistic community prior to the writing of the text.

I. Disciples, Harp, and Flute at Eucharist

I will suggest here that unusual aspects of the descriptions of
Mary Magdalene and the male disciples find their analogue in
Paul's description of speaking in tongues; and furthermore, that
a correct interpretation of their oddity functions as it does in 1
Corinthians 14, in tandem with more unambiguous prophetic
declarations concerning God's act in Christ.

We begin with the Pauline corpus and a particular musical discussion concerning harp and flute, *kithara and auloi*. In
1 Corinthians 14, Paul discusses the need to interpret the gift of

tongues, speech in the Spirit. In the course of making that case, he says in verse 7: "Similarly with lifeless instruments that produce sound, whether harp or flute; if I do not render clear articulation to the noises, how will the (tune of) the harp or flute be understood?" What proves so striking to the attentive reader of John 20 is that Jesus, Mary and the disciples are described as speaking and acting in ways analogous to those musical instruments!

First, listen carefully to the nature of her comment in verse 15b: "If you have taken him away, tell me where you have put him, and I will take him." I will take him? A woman, deeply sunk in grief, will take a literal dead-weight corpse? How? This simply doesn't work at the literal level, but the Evangelist has indeed emphasized it.[1] Her comment mimics the almost-identical one in verse 13, but verse 15 adds the *arō*, I will take. Note that the words of verse 15 **kyrie-eth**ēkas—**arō** contain within them a reminder of the *kithara* which Mary somehow instantiates.[2] Note further how the diction of the passage contributes to that portrait. The story is replete with discussion of *aggeloi/gynai/aggelousa* (vss. 12, 13, 15,18) The guttural *g* is, of all the other possible phonetic expressions (labial, dental, palatal), the one that most fully employs the vocal chords. Even as the reader reads aloud the text of these verses, the vocal chords are at work in much the same fashion as the strings of a harp. It is in that context that one should hear verse 15's *k-eth-arō* as a visual reminder of the separate strings of the harp that Mary somehow is. Indeed, these components are evenly spaced at a distance from one another, as is the case with the strings of a harp.

Most commentators recognize that, in the resurrection appearances of 20:11-18, Jesus is not in the same mode of being

---

1. Keener, *Gospel of John*, 2.1190 emphasizes the "tremendous physical effort" involved.

2. I justify this kind of observation on the basis of verses such as John 6:51, 54 that elicit the hearer's *chewing* of the Word enfleshed. And I am assuming that the text is an instantiation of that same Word. In the fourth century, Augustine will also discuss *chewing the word* along with the eucharistic bread. See the discussion in Tillard, *Flesh of the Church*, 130.

as was the historical Jesus.[3] I would suggest that describing the mode he does occupy is greatly helped by attention to musicology. We may get an inkling of his transformed state when we remember that the word *haptō* (in "do not hold on to me" vs. 17) can mean "fasten a lyre string" and is so used when Homer describes the return of *Odysseus* in the Odyssey.[4] The seventeenth verse continues in part "for I have not yet ascended" and "Go to my brothers and tell them I am ascending. . . ." I think it apposite to see here the exaltation of the crown of the lyre, Jesus. In this new mode of being, he is inviting Mary Magdalene, as the stringed instrument she has become in him, to employ her vocal chords in announcing his word to the community.

And listen to Jesus interacting with the male disciples: He breathed (*emphysao*) into them (vs. 22), and said to Thomas "Put your finger here, put your hand into my side" (vs. 27). First, note the aspirative dimension of his communication: *hagion* and *hamartias* both require the prominent expulsion of breath. In this context, one remembers that the *auloi* were supported by the thumb, and the notes were delineated by splaying the four other fingers along the holes on its side. And it was not uncommon that two *auloi*, not just one, were played at a time.[5] Note that Thomas is designated in verse 24 as Didymus, *the Twin* and, in the same verse, his distinction from the other (*alloi*) disciples underscored. Note as well that the invited extension of Thomas' hand functions as a synecdoche both of Jesus' holding onto his own (6:37, 39; 10:27–29; 17:12; 18:9) and of the disciples holding

---

3. Schneiders, *Written That You May Believe* 197–201.

4. "But the man skilled in all ways of contending (Odysseus), satisfied by the great bow's look and heft, like a musician, like a harper, when with quiet hand upon his instrument, he draws between his thumb and forefinger, a sweet new string upon a peg. . . . Bk 21. 404–8.

5. See Grove "Aulos" in *Grove's Dictionary of Music and Musicians*. The fresco at Herculaneum depicts a rendition on the double *aulos*. See Wellesz, *Ancient and Oriental Music*, 414. Also see Braun, *Music in Ancient Israel/ Palestine*.

onto one another (20:23b).[6] The auletic metaphor would suggest that the community confessing Jesus as Lord also holds onto all of those who are drawn into making that confession, both early and late.

One should note that the Evangelist's agenda follows the appropriate cues of number and gender proffered by these instruments: the singular feminine *kithara* interwoven into Mary's narrative;[7] the plural masculine *auloi* into that of the male disciples.

But why would the Evangelist embark on such a seemingly odd venture? I think that the answer resides in the way in which the Thomas episode functions in relation to the rest of the narratives. Thomas' confession "My Lord and my God" is spoken by someone who is evangelized by the other disciples (20:25). He then describes himself and is characterized by Jesus as unbelieving (20:25, 27). Compare this imagined scenario in 1 Corinthians 14:24, 25:

> But if all are prophesying when an unbelieving
> outsider comes in, he is convicted by all,
> he is judged by all, the secrets of his heart are
> laid bare, and so he will fall on his face and
> worship God, declaring that God truly is among you.

I would suggest that the unusual cited contours of the narratives of Mary Magdalene and the male disciples function, like tongues, as language to be interpreted, whose intended meaning

---

6. Schneiders, "The Resurrection," 186–87 translates John 20:23b as, "whomever you hold, are held fast."

7. The fresco at Herculaneum, already referenced above in note 5, depicts a male player of the auloi and a female player of the kithara. Mary as kitharist may also generate the motif of her weeping, a peculiarly Johannine feature (John 20:11,13,15). Commentators are in considerable agreement that Pss. 41–42 LXX have influenced the diction of the Gospel at several points: e.g., Hanson, *Prophetic Gospel*. But in addition one may note that Ps. 42 LXX says, "I will praise you on the kithara, O God my God; why are you downcast, and why are you disturbed within me? Hope in God; I will yet praise him, my Savior and God."

is not immediately self-evident. They function in a position of secondary importance compared to that of the prophetic dynamics of the chapter calling for belief. But they are an indispensable part of John's language in the Spirit, the language needed to convey the mystery of Jesus glorified. Like tongues, the metaphorical language of the Fourth Evangelist is odd at first hearing but also like tongues, is accompanied by rather precise confessional formulae.[8] In reflecting on the believing assembly, both Paul and John turn to a presentation of these two common musical instruments to accompany the articulate confession of God's presence among them.[9] 1 Corinthians 12:3 even links the name Jesus to the title "Lord" as does John 20:28. The major difference in the Pauline and Johannine presentations resides in the fact that one is hortatory while one is worked out in narrative fashion.

II. God's Singing Image at Eucharist

John 20 is even more fully explicable when one steps outside the realm of the undisputed Pauline corpus and enters the Deutero-Pauline corpus. There, in Colossians 1:15–20, Christ is presented as "image of the invisible God" and, in his members, as singing songs of thanksgiving (Col 3:15–17). Both of those dynamics are pertinent to John 20.

8. Johnson, "Glossolalia," pursues the interesting suggestion that Paul's critique of tongues' excess is tied to a concern for the activity of women prophets in Corinth. No such concern is evident in the Fourth Gospel, whose Mary Magdalene functions as revered *aggelos* (20:18).

9. Note too Paul's concern in 1 Cor 12:2 that the community remember that its speech should indicate its detachment from dumb idols. This is another example of the symmetry between the situations of the two communities: the hands of the Johannine Jesus act, *ex hypothese*, as critique of the lifeless idols of Ps. 115. See more below.

John 20 and the image of God

To the deutero-Pauline portrait of Christ as image of the invisible God, compare John's portrait of Jesus displaying his vivified hands. Jesus displays hands and side to the assembled male disciples (vss. 20, 27). This act of displaying his animated hands is best understood, I think, in light of a portrait such as that in Psalm 115:7. There the idols of the nations are mocked for having hands, but ones that do not feel. In contrast, I would suggest, Jesus is presented by the Evangelist here as remote from such dead idols and instead as imaging the living God.[10]

One of the best indices for gauging the propriety of this interpretation resides in the last verse of 1 John, a letter that Raymond Brown has suggested is meant as a guide to proper interpretation of the Gospel. It says tersely, "Little children, be on your guard against idols" (1 John 5:21).[11]

John 20 and Psalms of Thanksgiving

The 'Christ' is defined in Colossians 3:15–17 as replete with many members who collectively sing "psalms, hymns, and spiritual songs" (the latter, *ōdais*) in the process of thanking the Father through him. With this, compare John's interweaving of Psalms of praise and thanksgiving into the narrative of John 20.

Psalm 22, which was used in the narrative of Jesus' lifting up (John 19:24), says in its twenty-second verse "I will tell of your name to my brothers, *in the midst* (*en mesō*) of the congregation I will praise you." Compare Jesus' words in John 20:17 "Go to my brothers and say to them, 'I ascend to my Father and your Father,

---

10. In John, hands and side are displayed together. But the hands and side function differently. The side, from which blood and water flowed, allude to his humanity.

11. Brown, *The Epistles*, 640 correlates the warning against idols with the confession of Thomas, though he does not isolate Ps. 115 in making this comment.

to my God and your God.'" In the ensuing scene, he stands "in the midst" (*eis to meson*) of the disciples (vs. 19).

Moreover, Psalm 122, a Psalm celebrating the act of going to Jerusalem to give thanks to the Name of the Lord, may have had a formative influence on the diction of verses 19–22. It twice repeats its prayer for the peace of Jerusalem; "Peace be within your walls" (Ps. 122:7) and "I will say 'Peace be within you'" (Ps. 122:8). Compare Jesus' appearance in Jerusalem and his twice-repeated greeting of peace in verses 19 and 21. There is a peculiar propriety as well to the use of this Psalm in the section immediately following Jesus' announced ascent (*anabainein*) in verse 17; Psalm 122 is one of the Psalter's Songs of Ascent (*anabathmōn*).

If in fact the Evangelist has subtly tailored the narratives in the direction of having the divine Name glorified, the process would be akin to that employed by the ancient rhapsodists (cf. *ōdais*) who interwove bits and snatches of earlier poetic works in their celebration of the heroes.

Summary and Conclusion

The foregoing data suggest in one instance some congruence between the exercise of tongues as described in the Pauline literature and hypothetically metaphorical language in this section of John. In John's use of the traditions in the undisputed Pauline corpus, we seem to have witness to ecstatic experience in Jesus' Spirit accompanied by a rendering of that experience in language that is, on the one hand, out of the ordinary, but that in both cases is complemented by intelligible, prophetic proclamations of Jesus in relation to the names/titles Lord and God.[12] In the second instance, that of John's use of the traditions of the deutero-Pauline corpus and selected Psalms, Christ is presented as image of God who sings songs of thanksgiving. What these readings share is an appreciation of the music of the pericopae. And I would suggest that one of the

12. For relevant theories about the sociological functions of language comprehended most fully by an "in-group," see Neyrey, "The Sociology," 79–110.

reasons for preferring a musicological reading of the Johannine dynamics resides in the oddly compelling beauty arising out of its power to hold together so many aspects of John 20.

The text of John 20, in short, offers a new twist on an old idea: Jesus Christ is not simply an individual any more. Christ, the image of God, cannot be fully comprehended apart from his members. And when those members witness and sing, they present to themselves and to the world their beloved Head.

seven

Acts 4–8 and Virgil's *Georgics*

AT THE TURN OF the millennium, Lukan commentary experienced an infusion of new energy in its discernment of the interaction of Luke-Acts with the work of Virgil.[1] Most critical commentaries contain at least a handful of suggested parallels to the *Aeneid*, as well as to the *Fourth Eclogue*. Partly on the basis of Georgic influence on *Revelation*, Aubert suggests that, "Similarly, it can be argued that Luke-Acts shows interest in the natural world, even though it is secondary and derived from literary sources."[2] In this essay, I explore in a more thoroughgoing way the relation of the *Georgics* to the early chapters of Acts. I thus identify Luke along with Q. Caecilius Epirota as early educators and writers who appreciated Virgil's *Georgics*.[3] There are more than a few remarkable congruities that exist between *Georgics* 4 and Acts 4–8.

The current level of Georgic commentary has become increasingly extensive and sophisticated. One recent commentary runs to almost one thousand pages.[4] Most commentators agree that Virgil's tale of the cultivation of the land is at one level an exhortation to embody the virtues of the rustic life throughout the renovated republic of Octavian Augustus. However, the part of Georgic commentary with which this essay is most congenial

1. Bonz, *The Past as Legacy*.
2. Aubert, *The Shepherd-Flock Motif in the Miletus Discourse*, 67n59.
3. Tarrant "Aspects of Virgil's Reception in Antiquity."
4. Erren, *Vergilius Maro, Georgica*.

is that of Dorothea Wender, who has suggested that resurrection or regeneration is the dominant theme of the fourth Georgic.[5] I am suggesting that the Evangelist explicates the results of Jesus' resurrection using two complementary frameworks: he uses certain aspects of the fourth Georgic while simultaneously rendering a narrative version of the parable of the Sower in Luke 8:4–15. These observations do not materially affect the current debate about the genre of Acts as a whole.[6] I am merely suggesting that the Evangelist allows for his story of the early church to be viewed within these two matrices. I am making no firm judgment about the historicity of the material that appears in these early chapters of Acts.

Parable of the Sower

We turn our attention first to the implicit presence of the parable. The events of Acts 4–8 detail the growth of the gospel and resistance thereto in the early Jerusalem and Samaritan communities. And that process of growth and threat-to-growth is what is shared between Acts 4–8 and the parable of the Sower.

In what ways are the various soils of Luke 8 exemplified in Acts 4–8? One type of soil allows no place for the seed to grow; no faith in the word occurs at all. Compare that with Acts 4:1–4 in which the crowd's response of faith in the word preached by Peter and John is met with threats and imprisonment. So too, Stephen's presentation in chapter 7 evokes a lethal anger in 7:53. Another kind of reaction to the word is initial joy, followed by a withering under persecution. We have an antitype to that process in the bravery of persecuted Peter and John in 5:17–42, and Stephen who is valiant to the death in 7:1—8:3. Another reaction to the word is preempted in its growth by worry, money, and pleasures. Money as such is the issue in the story of the greedy

---

5. Wender, "Resurrection in the Fourth Georgic."
6. Phillips, "The Genre of Acts."

couple in Acts 5:1–11 as well as in the attempt of Simon to purchase the Spirit's power in 8:4–25. Finally, some seed falls into good and generous hearts that bear fruit in patience. Barnabas fits this description, in his giving to the apostles the proceeds of a sale of land (4:36, 37), an early harbinger of a fruitful ministry with Paul in 11:24 and following. One might also see the scattering of the church of Jerusalem into surrounding regions, and the immediately ensuing notice of the burial of Stephen (8:1, 2) as analogous to the broadcasting of seed and its falling into the earth presupposed in the parable of Luke 8.

Even Azotus (8:40) is a fitting conclusion to the presence of the seed parable in Acts 4–8. Azotus is located in the fertile Shephelah region along the coast of southern Palestine. It constitutes the geographical component in Acts' larger rendition of the fruitful Word in Luke 8. As the Spirit animated something like wind and fire at Pentecost, and as the Spirit has just fructified the water of Acts 8, so now the Spirit will increasingly draw harvest from the land.

Georgics 4

What occurs in Acts 8:26–40 is akin to a miracle of nature described in Georgics 4. I refer to the *bougonia*, a spontaneous generation of bees from the carcass of a slain ox. The text of Isaiah, quoted at Acts 8:32, 33, includes this line about the one unjustly slain: "who will recount his generation?" Or more paraphrastically in the NAB "who will tell of his posterity?" Surprising generations of life-from-death, distinct in their own ways, are shared by both the sacred and secular authors. Indeed, commentators are agreed that there is little attention to redemption as such in the Isaiah text quoted by Luke, and I would suggest that once he announces the theme of *generation*, he has achieved his primary Christological goal in this part of the narrative. Indeed, Luke has prepared his hearers to understand his agenda by having Peter cite a Scripture attending to Jesus as *gōnia*, corner(stone) in Acts

4:11. By shaping the contours of his narrative in Acts 4–8 along the lines of the parable of the Sower, Luke has in part portrayed a nature miracle of life-from-death, and in that regard one similar to the Virgilian miracle of *bougonia*, whose name he adumbrates as he opens the section in Acts 4.

While that portrayal constitutes what I think is one of the most delightful and surprising dimensions of Luke's agenda, it is complemented by other dynamics similar to those in Georgics 4, a book largely concerned with bees who display behavior analogous to that of humans. Luke has studied the portrait well. Here are some of the most striking parallels[7]

a) The relation in Acts 8 between the royal Candace of Ethiopia and the eunuch in charge of her treasury has its analogue in the royal bee attended by asexual drones in Georgics 4.197–209.

b) Virgil's bees are celebrated for their love of the *glory* of honey-making (*tantus amor . . . generandi gloria mellis* 4.205). And the twin stories of *grief* in the epyllion (the miniature epic) of that book, the tales of Aristaeus and Orpheus /Euridice, take place in the narrative space between two descriptions of the *bougonia*. So too, Stephen's description of God's *glory* in his vision (7:55) and the *threnody* raised by Stephen's friends over his corpse in 8:2, are framed by the Lukan *bougonia* which culminates in Acts 8, but which begin to appear on the horizon in Acts 4.[8]

c) In his quest to assuage his grief over the loss of his swarm of bees, the Aristaeus just mentioned is guided by his goddess mother through an explanation that highlights injustice and that culminates in his enacting the ritual of *bougonia*. On his way to that moment, he is submerged in a pool of water that gives him access to the Underworld

7. Miles, *Virgil's Georgics* 226–94.
8. Nappa, "Puzzles of Glory and Grief," 160–218.

(Georgics 4.359–73). The eunuch of Acts 8: 36–39 seeks baptism after his encounter with Philip's description of life-from-unjust-death. There is even a formal correspondence between the eunuch's three questions and the same number of questions asked by Aristaeus at *Georgics* 4.320–330.

d) Virgil presents *bougonia* as a mystery having its origins in Egypt (4.287–94). In part, this celebrates the victory of Octavian in Egypt over the forces of Marc Antony and Cleopatra. So it should not be surprising that of the fourteen times that the word "Egypt" occurs in Acts, twelve occurrences are in Stephen's speech in Acts 7. The Acts account emphasizes attendant signs and wonders (7:36; as also at 5:12–16).

e) The setting of the Georgics is the recently ended civil war that brought Octavian to power. Consider in this light the focus on civil unrest in Acts 4:23–28 and the fact that Stephen's speech concludes with mention of Solomon whose career, like that of Octavian, was caught up in civil war.

f) On excursions outside the hive, Virgil's bees take up little stones for ballast (4.195–96). Stephen's hearers drag him outside the city to stone him (Acts 7:58).

g) Virgil's bees (4.157) surrender their acquisitions to the common use. Consider in this regard notices of communal sharing and the gift of Barnabas (Acts 4:32–37).[9]

h) The bees share in divine reason, as exemplified in their division of labor (4.158–68). Consider in this light the decision of the apostles to attend to the word and prayer while assigning the task of serving at table to others (Acts 6:1–7).

---

9. For a comparison of the Georgics with the political philosophies of Seneca and Cicero, see Dahlmann, "Der Bienenstaat in Vergil's Georgica."

i) The concentration on bees (L. *apes*) in Georgics 4 is mirrored in Luke's attention to *apostoloi*. Of the thirty occurrences of *apostolos* in the twenty-eight chapters of Acts, fourteen occur in Acts 4–8.

j) Aristaeus is described as a bold youth at *Georgics* 4.445 (*iuvenum confidentissimus*). In context, this surely was meant to recall the young Octavian to Virgil's readers and finds an echo in the believers' prayer for boldness in Acts 4:23–31.

k) The final vision of the Georgics describes a new swarm of bees "hanging from a tree" near the slain carcass of an ox. Compare the similar motif in Peter's speech at Acts 5:30 "whom you killed, hanging him on a tree".

l) At 4.294 Virgil asserts, "all the country places sure relief *salum* in this art" (the rite of *bougonia*). This description of the rite as saving in some sense functions as a partial analogue to the emphasis on salvation in Acts 4–8 (savior at 4:12, 5:31, 7:25; salvation at 4:12, 7:25), though salvation is emphasized elsewhere in Luke-Acts as well.

m) Perhaps one of the most intriguing linguistic dynamics attached to Luke's use of Georgics is the fact that the word for *swarm* (L. *examen*) can also mean *crowd* and *investigation*. Within Acts 4–8, we see 5:12–16 describing the former. The investigation of 4:6, corresponds to the latter sense. And the cognate word *examino*, weigh or deliberate, finds its parade exemplification in Gamaliel's careful elucidation of the options to be considered in responding to the new movement (5:34–42).

n) Augustus' friend Gallus who was installed but then removed from office in Egypt has his analogue in the narrative about the replacement of Judas in Acts 1:12–26. Some critics assert that the *epyllion* of Aristaeus and Orpheus/Euridice now comprising the latter half of book four is a tribute to Gallus' poetic accomplishments in the same literary endeavor.[10] I draw attention only to the fact that the Judas narrative opens the Evangelist's second text, Acts, while the *epyllion* constitutes the second portion of Georgics 4.

o) If one grants the plausibility of these purported links, one may read at least three aspects of the Gospel of Luke as anticipating the discussion in Acts of Jesus and *bougonia*. Only Luke 15:23 among the canonical Gospels discusses the fatted calf. The Vulgate at this point uses the same term, *vitulus*, as occurs in *Georgics* 4.290–310. Among the canonical Gospels, only Luke has Jesus on the cross make explicit mention of his *spirit:* "Father, into your hands I commit my spirit" (Luke 23:46a). In this regard, note that the ritual bull in *Georgics* 4.290–310 is subjected to death-by-suffocation. Moreover, some manuscripts of Luke 24:42 have the risen Jesus eating "fish and a portion of honeycomb." I would suggest that those scribes correctly intuited the program of *bougonia* in Acts, and in Luke 24 have begun to prepare for it.

p) Of the three occurrences of *euchē* in the New Testament, two occur in Acts (18:18, 21:23). This constitutes part of a handful of occurrences of words in Acts having initial *euch* (*eucharistia* 24:3; *eucharisteo* 27:35, 28:15; *euchomai* 27:29, 28:29). Should we see the story of *Aristaeus* in *Georgics* 4 as one of the sources of the Evangelist's meditation on the Eucharistic meals of his church?

Conclusion

I offer two speculations that may add a more substantial horizon to these close readings. What then are we to say about Luke's

10. Coleman, "Gallus, the Bucolics, and the Ending of the Fourth Georgic," 297.

appropriation of a secular poet for his narrative? I would suggest that in his frequent use of Isaiah, Luke has already signaled to his hearers that his narrative, like that of the prophet who celebrated the secular ruler Cyrus of Persia, is also open to the non-Israelite world as venue of God's action. Moreover, the Latin *vates* means both poet and prophet. We might well entertain the possibility that Luke thinks of Virgil as a secular prophet who is to some degree useful in articulation of the gospel.

Secondly, traditional iconography of Luke presents him as an ox. Without prejudice to the many valid insights often brought forward to justify that portrait from the Jewish Scriptures, I would suggest that the rite of *bougonia* was an equally strong factor in production of the Lukan image.

Bibliography

Adler, Yonatan. "Identifying Sectarian Characteristics in the Phylacteries from Qumran." *Revue de Qumran* 89:23 (2007) 79–92.

Anderson, Janice Capel. "Feminist Criticism: The Dancing Daughter." In *Mark and Method: New Approaches in Biblical Studies*," 103–34. Minneapolis: Fortress, 1992.

Arterbury, Andrew E. "Breaking the Betrothal Bonds: Hospitality in John 4" *Catholic Biblical Quarterly* 72:1 (2010) 63–83.

Aubert, Bernard. *The Shepherd-Flock Motif in the Miletus Discourse (Acts 20:17–38) Against Its Historical Background.* New York: Peter Lang, 2009.

Bonner, Stanley Frederick. *Education in Ancient Rome.* Berkeley: University of California Press, 1977.

Bonz, Marianne Palmer. *The Past as Legacy: Luke-Acts and Ancient Epic.* Minneapolis: Fortress, 2000.

Bovon, Francois *Luke 1: A Commentary on Luke 1:1—9:50.* Hermeneia. Minneapolis: Augsburg Fortress, 2002.

Bradley, Marshell Carl. *Matthew: Poet, Historian, Dialectician.* New York: Peter Lang, 2007.

Braun, Joachim. *Music in Ancient Israel/Palestine: Archaeological, Written, and Comparative Sources.* Grand Rapids: Eerdmans, 2002.

Brodie, Louis T. "A New Temple and a New Law: The Unity and Chronicler-based Nature of Luke 1:1—4:22a." *Journal for the Study of the New Testament* 5 (1979) 21–45.

Brown, Raymond E. *The Birth of the Messiah: A Commentary on the Infancy Narratives in the Gospels of Matthew and Luke.* The Anchor Yale Bible Reference Library. Garden City, NY: Doubleday, 1999.

———. *The Epistles of John.* Vol. 40, The Anchor Bible. Garden City, NY: Doubleday, 1982.

Burchard, Christopher. *Der Jakobusbrief.* Tubingen: Mohr-Siebeck, 2000.

Charlesworth, James H. *The Old Testament Pseudepigrapha.* Vol. 2 Garden City, NY: Doubleday, 1985.

Coleman, Robert. "Gallus, the Bucolics, and the Ending of the Fourth Georgic." In *Virgil: Critical Assessments of Classical Authors*, edited by Philip Hardie, 2.289–300. New York: Routledge, 1999.

Collins, John N. "Re-thinking 'Eyewitnesses' in the Light of 'Servants of the Word' (Luke 1:2)." *Expository Times* 121:9 (2010) 447–52.

Bibliography

Cribiore, Raffaella. *Gymnastics of the Mind: Greek Education in Hellenistic and Roman Egypt.* Princeton: Princeton University Press, 2001.

Dahlmann, H. "Der Bienenstaat in Vergil's Georgica." In *Virgil: Critical Assessments of Classical Authors,* edited by Philip Hardie, 2.253–67. New York: Routledge, 1999.

Davies, W D and Dale C. Allison. *A Critical and Exegetical Commentary on the Gospel According to St. Matthew.* 3 vols. International Critical Commentary. Edinburgh: T&T Clark, 1988–1997.

Ellis, Peter F. *Matthew: His Mind and his Message.* Collegeville MN: Liturgical Press, 1974.

Endres, John C. "The Spiritual Vision of Chronicles: Wholehearted, Joy-Filled Worship of God." *Catholic Biblical Quarterly* 69:1 (2007) 1–21.

Erren, Manfred, and P. Vergilius Maro. P. *Vergilius Maro, Georgica: Einleitung, Praefatio, Text und Übersetzung.* Heidelberg: Winter., 2003.

Fitzgerald, Robert, trans. *Homer: The Odyssey.* Garden City, NY: Anchor/Doubleday, 1961.

Freedman, David Noel, ed. "Phylacteries," in *The Anchor Bible Dictionary* (Garden City, NY: Doubleday, 1992), 5.368–70.

Friedlander, P. "Pattern of Sound and Atomistic Theory in Lucretius." In *Oxford Readings in Lucretius,* edited by Monica Gale, 351–70. New York: Oxford University Press, 2007.

Glucker, John "Cicero's Philosophical Associations." In *The Question of Eclecticism: Studies in Later Greek Philosophy,* edited by John M. Dillon and A. A. Long, 34–59. Berkeley; University of California Press, 1988.

Green, Jonathon. *Chasing the Sun: Dictionary-Makers and the Dictionaries They Made.* London: Cape, 1996.

Green, Joel B. "The Problem of a Beginning: Israel's Scriptures in Luke 1–2." *Bulletin for Biblical Research* 4 (1994) 61–86.

Grove, George and Stanley Sadie "Aulos." In *The New Grove's Dictionary of Music and Musicians.* Washington DC: Grove's Dictionaries of Music, 1980.

Hamm, Dennis. "The Tamid Service in Luke-Acts: the Cultic Background behind Luke's Theology of Worship (Luke 1:5–25; 18:9–14; 24:50–53; Acts 3:1; 10:3, 30)" *Catholic Biblical Quarterly* 65:2 (2003) 215–31.

Hanson, Anthony Tyrrell. *The Prophetic Gospel: Study of John and the Old Testament.* Edinburgh: T&T Clark, 1991.

Hayward, C.T. Robert "Guarding Head and Heel: Observations on Septuagint Genesis 3:15." In *Studies in the Greek Bible: Essays in Honor of Francis T. Gignac,* edited by Jeremy Corley et al., 17–34. Catholic Biblical Quarterly Monograph Series 44. Washington, DC: Catholic University Press, 2008.

Johnson, Luke T. "Glossolalia and the Embarrassments of Experience." In *Religious Experience in Earliest Christianity: A Missing Dimension in New Testament Studies,* 105–36. Minneapolis: Fortress, 1998.

Joyal, Mark et al. *Greek and Roman Education: A Sourcebook.* London: Routledge, 2009.

Jung, Chang-Wook. *The Original Language of the Lukan Infancy Narrative.* Journal For The Study of the New Testament Supplement Series, 267. London: T&T Clark, 2004.

Kasper, Walter. *That They All May be One: The Call to Unity Today.* London: Burns and Oates, 2004.

Keener, Craig S. "'Brood of Vipers' (Matthew 3.7; 12.34; 23.33)." *Journal for the Study of the New Testament* 28:1 (2005) 3–11.

———. *The Gospel of John: A Commentary.* 2 Vols. Peabody, MA: Hendrickson, 2003.

Kiley, Mark. "Law, Wisdom, and the Housing Crisis." In *Ideas of the Holy,* edited by Justus George Lawler, 309–24. New York: Continuum, 1993.

Kingsbury, Jack, ed. *Gospel Interpretation: Narrative-Critical and Social-Scientific Approaches.* Eugene, OR: Wipf and Stock, 2003.

———. *Matthew as Story.* Philadelphia: Fortress, 1988.

Kraemer, Ross S. "Implicating Herodias and Her Daughter in the Death of John the Baptizer: A (Christian) Theological Strategy?" *Journal of Biblical Literature* 125:2 (2006) 321–49.

Kuhn, Karl. "Beginning the Witness: The *autoptai kai hypēretai* of Luke's Infancy Narrative." *New Testament Studies* 49:2 (2003) 237–55.

Laws, Sophie. *A Commentary on the Epistle of James.* Black's New Testament Commentaries. London: Black, 1980.

McCartney, Dan G. *James.* Baker Exegetical Commentary. Grand Rapids: Baker Academic, 2009.

Marcus, Joel. *Mark 1–8: A New Translation with Introduction and Commentary.* New York: Doubleday, 2000.

Marrou, Henri I. *A History of Education in Antiquity.* Madison: University of Wisconsin Press, 1956.

Meier, John P. *A Marginal Jew: Rethinking the Historical Jesus.* Vol. 2, *Mentor, Message, Miracles.* New York: Doubleday, 1994.

Miles, Gary B. *Virgil's Georgics: A New Interpretation.* Berkeley: University of California Press, 1980.

Miller, Patrick. "Kingship, Torah Obedience, and Prayer: The Theology of Psalms 15–24." In *Israelite Religion and Biblical Theology: Collected Essays,* JSOT Supp 267. Sheffield, 2000.

Moloney, Francis J. "Mark 6:6b–30: Mission, the Baptist, and Failure." *Catholic Biblical Quarterly* 63:4 (2001) 647–63.

Müller, Robert, ed. *Varros Logistoricus über Kindererziehung.* Leipzig, 1938.

Murphy, Catherine M. *John the Baptist: Prophet of Purity for a New Age.* Collegeville, MN: Liturgical Press, 2003.

Nappa, Christopher. "Puzzles of Glory and Grief." In *Reading After Actium: Vergil's Georgics, Octavian and Rome.* 160–218. Ann Arbor: University of Michigan Press, 2005.

Narins, Brigham, ed. *The World of Mathematics.* Farmington Hills, MI: Thompson Gale, 2001.

Nebelsick, Harold P. *Circles of God: Theology and Science from the Greeks to Copernicus.* Edinburgh: Scottish Academic Group, 1985.

Neyrey, Jerome. "The Sociology of Secrecy and the Fourth Gospel." In vol. 2, *Literary and Social Readings of the Fourth Gospel,* edited by F. Segovia, 79–109. Atlanta: Scholars Press, 1998.

———. "What's Wrong with This Picture? John 4, Cultural Stereotypes of Women, and Public and Private Space." In vol. 1, *A Feminist Companion to John,* edited by Amy-Jill Levine and Marianne Blickenstaff, 98–125. New York: Sheffield Academic, 2003.

Nussbaum, Martha C. *The Therapy of Desire: Theory and Practice in Hellenistic Ethics.* Princeton University Press, 1994.

O'Brien, Kelli S. "Written That You May Believe: John 20 and Narrative Rhetoric." *Catholic Biblical Quarterly* 67:2 (2005) 284–302.

Ostler, Nicholas. *Ad Infinitum: A Biography of Latin.* New York: Walker, 2007.

Pennington, Jonathan. *Heaven and Earth in the Gospel of Matthew.* Leiden: Brill, 2007.

Phillips, Thomas E. "The Genre of Acts: Moving Toward a Consensus?" *Currents in Biblical Research* 4:3 (2006) 365–96.

Plummer, Alfred. *An Exegetical Commentary on the Gospel According to St. Matthew.* Grand Rapids: Eerdmans, 1956.

Poplutz, Uta. "Verunsicherter Glaube. Der finale Zweifel der Junger in Matthausevangelium aus figuranalytischer Sicht." In *Studien zu Matthäus und Johannes: Festschrift für Jean Zumstein zu seinem 65. Geburtstag,* edited by Andrea Detwiler and Uta Poplutz, 29–47. Zurich: TVZ, 2009.

Rothschild, Clare K. *Baptist Traditions and Q.* Tubingen: Mohr Siebeck, 2006.

Schneiders, Sandra. "The Resurrection (of the Body) in the Fourth Gospel: A Key to Johannine Spirituality." In *Life in Abundance: Studies of John's Gospel in Tribute to Raymond E. Brown,* edited by John Donahue, 168–98. Collegeville, MN: Liturgical Press, 2005.

———. *Written That You May Believe.* New York: Crossroad, 1999.

Scott, Spencer F. *Dancing Girls, Loose Ladies, and Women of the Cloth: The Women in Jesus' Life.* New York: Continuum, 2004.

Sihler, Andrew L. *A New Comparative Grammar of Greek and Latin.* New York: Oxford, 1995.

Sumi, Atsushi. "The Species *infima* as the Infinite: Timaeus 39e7–9, Parmenides 144b4–c1 and Philebus 16e1–2 in Plotinus Ennead VI.2.22." In *Reading Plato in Antiquity,* edited by Harold Tarrant and Dirk Baltzly. London: Duckworth, 2006.

Tarrant, R.J. "Aspects of Virgil's Reception in Antiquity." In *A Cambridge Companion to Virgil,* edited by Charles Martindale, 56–72. Cambridge: Cambridge University Press 1997.

Taylor, Daniel J. *Declinatio: A Study of the Linguistic Theory of Marcus Terentius Varro.* Amsterdam: John Benjamins, 1974.

Taylor, Joan E. *The Immerser: John the Baptist within Second Temple Judaism* Grand Rapids: Eerdmans, 1997.

Tillard, J -M -R. *Flesh of the Church, Flesh of Christ.* Collegeville, MN: Liturgical Press, 2001.

Torrell, Jean-Pierre. *St. Thomas Aquinas.* Vol. 2, *Spiritual Master,* translated by Robert Royal. Washington DC: Catholic University of America Press, 2003.

Webb, Robert L. *John the Baptizer and Prophet: A Socio-Historical Study.* Sheffield: JSOT, 1991.

Wellesz, Egon. *Ancient and Oriental Music.* London: Oxford, 1957.

Wender, Dorothea S. "Resurrection in the Fourth *Georgic.*" *The American Journal of Philology.*Vol. 90:4 (1969) 424–36.

Wheelock, Frederick M. *Latin: An Introductory Course Based on Ancient Authors.* New York: Barnes & Noble, 1963.

Wright, William M. IV. "Greco-Roman Character Typing and the Presentation of Judas in the Fourth Gospel." *Catholic Biblical Quarterly* 71:3 (2009) 544–59.

Yarbro Collins, Adela. *Mark: A Commentary.* Hermeneia. Minneapolis: Fortress, 2007.

Young, Frances. *A History of Biblical Interpretation.* Vol. 1. *The Ancient Period.* Edited by Alan J. Hauser and Diane Watson, 334-54. Grand Rapids: Eerdmans, 2003.

Index of Ancient Sources

ACTS OF THE APOSTLES

VIRGIL

Index of Modern Authors

Index of Modern Authors

Subject Index

Subject Index

commandments, 18,
  and soldiers (Matt 28), 19
covenant, 12, 15
cross of Jesus, 6, 16, 23, 48, 50, 59,
    60, 72
  as tree, 71
  titulus on , 40
David, 36,
  and pi in GMatt, 7
death of Jesus, 3
Decalogue at Qumran, 15
deutero-Pauline corpus
  and John 20, 64
doctoral dissertations,
  Catholic universities, xi
dowry in GJn, 48
earth in Matthew, 6
ecumenism, xiv
  and Fourth Gospel, 55–56
Egypt, 1, 23, 70
Eleven, The, 14
  and phylactery, 16
Emmaus, 39
diameter, 1
ecstatic experience in Sprit, 64
Emmanuel, 12
emotions, negative,
  and serpent imagery, 27
entrance liturgy,
  at Jerusalem Temple, xiii, 35
Epicurean, 24
Etruscan,
  and Latin, 47
etymology, popular, 30
Eucharist, xiv
  and Acts, 72
  and John , 57, 58–61, 62
  and Mark, 23n.8
Euclid, 1, 9
"Eureka" and Matthew, 9, 10
exegesis, rabbinic and Western
  biblical, ix
eyewitnesses,
  and 'Ayin in Luke, 28

expulsion from school, 53
"face" in Ps. 24
  of God, 38
  of Jacob, 39
flashback, 21
flute,
  double auloi
  and Didymus, 59, 60
forgiveness
  in Matthew, 7
  in Luke, 39
Galilaia and circle, 10
generation,
  posterity, 68
  of bees in Georgics, 68
generous hearts, 68
gerund and direct object,
  Peter and Beloved Disciple,
    50–51
glory, 34, 36, 37, 62, 69
good, true, beautiful, 47
grief
  and death (Gen 3), 22
gutturals
  and musical strings, 59
harp/lyre, 58–60
Hebrew, Greek, Latin, xi, 40
heavens, 6, 36
Hellenism, xi, 13
Herculaneum,
  fresco of harp & flute, 60, 61
Hermes, 4
Herod Antipas/Herodians, 21–26
history,
  and circle in GMatt, 4, 5
  and The Eleven in GMatt 16, 17
  in Mark 6, 21
  in Luke 1, 2, 29
  in John, 42
  in Acts, 67
Holy of Holies, 12
homiletics, 58
hundred-fold harvest,
  and "believe' in GJn, 50

Subject Index